Mother Angelica's Keys to the Interior Life

Also by Mother Angelica

Mother M. Angelica

Mother Angelica's Keys to the Interior Life

Edited by Laura Rachel Yanikoski

EWTN Publishing, Inc.
Irondale, Alabama

These chapters are taken from the *Mother Angelica Live* EWTN television program.

Copyright © 2024 by EWTN Publishing, Inc.

Printed in the United States of America. All rights reserved.

Cover design by LUCAS Art & Design, Jenison, MI.

On the cover: Our Lady of the Angels Monastery, Hanceville, Alabama.

Except where Mother Angelica paraphrases or quotes from memory, quotations from Holy Scripture are generally taken from the Jerusalem Bible, © 1966 by Darton Longman and Todd Ltd. and Doubleday and Company Ltd.

EWTN Publishing, Inc.
5817 Old Leeds Road, Irondale, AL 35210

Distributed by Sophia Institute Press, Box 5284, Manchester, NH 03108.

paperback ISBN 978-1-68278-393-1
ebook ISBN 978-1-68278-394-8

Library of Congress Control Number: 2024940867

Second printing

Contents

Part 1
Keys to Prayer

Part 2
Keys to the Spiritual Life

Part 1

KEYS TO PRAYER

Dryness in Prayer

Many of you have had the experience that when you pray, it seems like God just isn't listening. We call that *dryness* because that's what it is; it's just not consoling. Prayer seems to be dead. Did you ever talk to someone and you know he's not listening? You can tell because he answers a question you never asked. That's a good hint that the person is not listening. So it's like talking to a wall. And you don't get a response. Well, sometimes that is what prayer feels like. We call that dryness.

So all of you that have had that problem—and if you've ever prayed at all, you've got the problem—tonight I want to show you that dryness is a *blessing*, not a problem. And so you are *blessed* by God. So often in life, we take something that's a blessing and we think it's a curse. That is one of the saddest things in life. We do that with suffering. We take suffering as a curse, something that is of no value.

Every soul experiences dryness, and it's very confusing. Because the harder you strive to be holy, the more you pray, the more Jesus seems to take a trip, and you just wonder: *What am I doing wrong?* So it's a very strange phenomenon. The phenomenon is that Jesus draws us to a fire, which is His love, but we feel cold. The love of Jesus: it's a fire, like the sun. And you're trying so hard to get close to this fire, but you're freezing. You're freezing although the sun is bright, shiny, and warm. And you're confused: *If I'm getting closer to the fire, how come I feel so cold?* That's what we want to talk about.

We're going to make a comparison. So often we take divine love and compare it with human love and feel that divine love is the same. That's your first mistake. What is human love? Human love is a feeling, most of the time, until it becomes more pure and becomes a decision. Human love is something you feel good about, something that makes you lighthearted, something that you look forward to, because you've got bones and flesh that you can look at with your eyes and talk to and get a response. So now we conclude that divine love should be the same. No. The very fact that one is "human" and the other "divine" already separates the two loves drastically.

For example, if you were a mountain climber, you start down in the valley, and everything is just terrific. You can breathe easily. But the air is not pure down here. As you begin to climb, you get out of breath. The higher you get, the harder it is, so you've got to take some of your pack off and you've got to put on an oxygen tank, because the air is *too pure*. It can be painful, and it's very fatiguing. The higher you climb into the purity of air, the harder it is. So, the spiritual life and dryness are exactly the same principle. The more you go up to the mountain of God—for the finite creature you are, to be able to climb to the divine, you need to be able to breathe the same kind of air. Something has got to happen to you before you can climb to this point.

And this climb is lonely. Why? Because a lot of people will fall away; there are very few who will reach the top. Why? Because they want the human element more than pure air. So loneliness is one of the problems of dryness. Dryness brings loneliness. Why does God allow this?

Well, let me tell you, there's nothing like dryness to make the soul begin to seek God. Dryness makes you seek God. You're thirsting for God, and you can't find Him. The Canticle of Canticles talks about this. The bride goes out, and she tries to find the bridegroom. And the bridegroom is hidden behind a lattice. He's peeking from behind. He's peeking from here, then from over here, and she's seeking him. So dryness is like that. It makes you seek God.

But you know what it also does? It's a marvelous thing. Dryness is a kind of spiritual anesthetic. Those of you who have had high degrees of dryness for long periods of time will understand that it's like an anesthetic. You're kind of numb inside. Why? So that the Lord can work on your soul. No one can have an operation without anesthetic, not a deep one anyway.

Another thing that dryness does—or that we do, rather, in dryness—is to look backward. So there's a danger here for our memory. You begin to look back because you're absolutely sure you did something wrong. God must be punishing you for something. "Let's see, I know it must have been that sin I committed twenty-three years ago on December 10." Dryness really begins to purify your memory. And when you begin to purify your memory, as you begin to look back, you become repentant. Maybe you weren't repentant before. Forgiving. This makes you seek God. Suddenly, worldly things become distasteful to you. For some of you, before you knew Jesus, maybe you'd go to a bar, or maybe you would gossip, or whatever it was. But now, when you get into a worldly situation, you kind of draw back. If not physically, then interiorly; you just kind of recoil from this worldliness that suddenly seems so useless to you.

Some of you might say, "I've sure got the dryness, but I don't know if it comes from God." So now you ask yourself: *Is my dryness from God? Or is it from lukewarmness?* I'm going to give you some signs that will help you judge this yourself. If it comes from God, it will cause pain. If you're lukewarm, nothing causes you pain. You couldn't care less, really, if you know God. Dryness that is from God increases your thirst for God. What kind of pain does dryness cause? Do I get a headache? No, it isn't physical pain. It's that feeling of helplessness. The feeling of talking to someone and they don't listen, of asking for something and they don't care. It's a feeling of being separated and you don't know why. And that's pain. That very pain, though, increases your love, your thirst for God. And then suddenly things that are sinful become distasteful. And another sign is that you strive for virtue.

So I'm going to give you a little synopsis. If you've got dryness that comes from God, it causes pain; it increases your thirst; it makes sinful things distasteful; and you strive for virtue. Well, isn't that encouraging? You see, God hasn't left you.

Another aspect of dryness. Dryness isn't only the feeling of not being able to pray. There is also *dryness of mind.* Dryness of mind. What does that mean? Well, sometimes your memory used to be able to meditate. You had the most gorgeous thoughts in your mind. And suddenly God begins to play "hide-and-seek." Your meditations in the past were just glorious, and now, you can't even squeeze a single thought out. Or some of you that are charismatic, when you first knew Jesus, you were so enthusiastic, you were ready to conquer the world. And then one morning you got up and it was all gone, and you didn't care if the sun rose or not. Remember that anesthetic I was talking about? Your memory is dulled, and your emotions are gone. Why? It is be-cause you compare divine love with human love, and there's no comparison. God is trying to teach you that. That's all. How else are you going to learn?

So, dryness prunes the memory; it brings out those weaknesses that you're not aware of. As I get older, I become more aware of my weaknesses. That's God's pruning. Sometimes dryness gives us an exaggerated view of our faults. You hear some people say, "I've got more faults than anybody; I'm a greater sinner than anybody." Those who are in the light of God, it's just so bright. But those way over here somewhere couldn't care less, because they've got sunglasses on their soul. Now, as this dryness begins to purify and you're getting closer to the Sun, well, the darkness goes away and you begin to see. By the time you get really close, you begin to see even the little specks, where before you didn't see anything. I mean, you were living in such darkness, you could see nothing. But as you get closer, you begin to see even little tiny specks.

And then God prunes you. All of a sudden everybody around you seems unbearable: they've got so many faults, so many weaknesses. And you've got to fight and fight to practice virtue; it all seems so hard. But persevere. It's worth it.

There's still another kind of dryness: *dryness of heart*. That's a hard one. It's very hard because we're emotional people. God made us emotional; we want to love, want to be loved. But again, we're accustomed to love on the human level, so we think loving God is impossible. A lot of people say, "Look, I can't love God. I need somebody with skin on." He's got skin. Jesus is resurrected.

So we begin to think we can't love God, that it's impossible to love God, when in reality He's the only one you really can love, because His love flows out. The love of husband and wife is only everlasting love if it is built on the love of God. The love of God is so important for us to survive, to live, because we were created by love and for love.

Now, my friends, and this is going to be a shock for some of you, but love is fed by sacrifice. You don't want to hear that, but it's true. Somewhere along the line, whether you love God or your neighbor, you've got to love on a decision level. People are friends because they share the same goals, the same ideals, the same love. And God draws them together. But even human love is chastised and cleansed by God. Whether your love is for your husband, your wife, your children, your relatives, or your friends, it must be cleansed. If not, it will breed selfishness. Both human love and divine love must be purified of selfishness. And that's why so many people when they get married, they're all lovey-dovey, they're perfect for each other, and then five, six months later, nothing. Why? Because their love on an emotional level couldn't take the dryness of human love.

There's dryness in human love and dryness in divine love, and the purpose is the same. When a man and a woman love each other on a will level, their love increases, because they're not loving for selfish reasons. They're wanting to give the other love, and so they're willing to suffer more to be able to *give* more. That's true of divine love too. The Lord does not want a love that is forced. Or a love that is only love when everything is hunky-dory, everything is perfect. What happens when my faults get on your nerves and my faults aggravate you? You don't love me then?

So dryness leads to detachment. And what is detachment? Is it indifference? No. It means you're able to love totally. Some of you are so afraid, "Oh, if I love God, He's going to take everything away from me." For goodness' sake! Detachment only means that my love is no longer selfish. Detachment leads to perfect love. We think that to be detached means I no longer love people. That's not detachment. That's stupidity. If you don't love, you dry up like a prune. Dryness separates our need for feeling; it exercises our will to love. So I can go to prayer, and I don't care if I *feel* anything; I go because I love. So you can go home to your wife tonight, and you don't care if her hair is all messed up, because you go to love.

So now, dryness leads to humility. How? In a dry period, you feel helpless. You feel absolutely devastated; there is nothing you can do, nothing you can think. You can try to read, but nothing. You're helpless. It increases your dependence upon God. It crushes our pride to the ground, but it also makes us realize how great God is.

Dryness also leads to patience. Why? Because you're forced to wait. There's nothing you can do; you've got to wait upon the Lord to come upon you, to manifest Himself again, to give you again the thought about Himself, to make you feel loved again. So you feel so helpless.

Dryness also strengthens us to persevere. I went to buy a piece of tile yesterday, and the woman in the store said, "No, you can't have that for under a stove. It's too hot. You've got to have one that's been tempered and fired to a high degree." And I went and looked, and it was true. I could bend it. In a fire, it would have melted. So dryness makes us strong because we love God always, without any hindrance as to feelings, thoughts, nothing.

And that's why it leads to a high degree of prayer. Why does it do that, you wonder? If I can't even pray at all in this dryness, how can it give me a high degree of prayer? Well, the highest degree of prayer is a kind of no-thought prayer, the kind of prayer where you can sit before the Lord and be totally content just to love. Without feelings. Without thought. Without assurance. Just there. This prayer is a gaze: you are looking, and you are content with that. This type of prayer gives you great strength in times of trial because you've been tempered. You know, a lot of people say they want to grow in prayer, but they don't progress, because they balk against dryness. They're going to fight it tooth and nail. And if they're charismatic, they'll run from one prayer group to another to get on a high. But once you begin to love God, free and pure, you begin to climb. And as you get to that mountain where your mind and your heart are pure, you don't need a thought; you don't need to have consolation. And when you begin to love God freely, you begin to enter into God. So you're no longer outside. Dryness takes you and brings you right inside. Dryness creates a vacuum, so that only God means everything to you.

Dryness gives you a proper perspective on the difference between yourself and God. It also gives you the understanding and the power to know the difference between yourself and your neighbor. Did you ever notice that when you feel very secure, and God is with you, and you feel all these consolations, how easy it is to find fault with your neighbors? But dryness keeps you from doing that. Dryness makes you aware of the beam that is in your own eye. What you see in your neighbor's eye is only a splinter. It takes dryness to make you know that. Dryness is the most wonderful tool that God has ever given us.

Now, dryness does something else: it increases my thirst for God and my desire for holiness. It makes you practice the Beatitudes. It is dryness that makes you poor in spirit. It is this suffering in spirit that makes you more compassionate. If you have gone through the real deep purification of dryness, you appreciate suffering; you appreciate it in other people. You know what else it does? It teaches you to hold the hand of God, to be able to pray without ceasing.

Dryness makes you seek God. It detaches you from selfishness. It makes you understand your neighbor. It gives you peace of mind because you're not obsessed by the desire for feeling. Dryness does all of this.

Sometimes, in dryness, we have a cry of desolation. It makes us cry out, "Oh, God, help me!" It makes us so dependent; it makes us so aware of our limitations. It strengthens our faith and hope, empties our self-indulgence, our selfishness, our conceit, our caustic temperament, our anger.

It takes our mind and begins to work on our understanding. It empties our intellect of doubt: *Does God love me?* You have no more doubt because you're no longer dependent on feeling. You *know*. Dryness increases faith.

And because you've got to keep pushing and pushing and pushing and pushing to continue to love God, suddenly you find that your will is very strong. So you don't need to worry about being lukewarm anymore. It's like putting a piece of iron in the fire. I used to work for a roller-bearing company, and I watched them pour this boiling iron into ingots. Dryness is the furnace of love. It never ceases to be a furnace, and it never ceases to be love. And so it purifies. Blessed the person who perseveres to the end. To the end. As we go along in our spiritual life, we have to come to that great decision: *Am I for God or against Him?* You know, in this day and age, we really don't know what comes tomorrow. We need to be vigilant, as St. Paul says. We don't know the time of Our Lord's coming or the time of our leaving.

Now, I just want to read you something:

Sometimes I'm so cold and in such darkness, I merely look to heaven, and that's a prayer of faith. And sometimes I'm perplexed and suffering and in pain and without comfort, and I say, "Thy will be done." And that's the prayer of resignation. And sometimes I feel such a failure and I want to improve, but I look to God alone to make me holy. And that's a prayer of humility. And sometimes I pray the prayer of the Church, sometimes I feel like everything is lost and I put my trust in God, and that's the prayer of hope. And sometimes I'm overwhelmed with joy, and I say, "Thank you Jesus." And that's a prayer of thanksgiving. And then there's sometimes I'm aware of His presence in the very depths of my soul, unseen, unfelt, and yet in some mysterious way tangible. And that's a prayer of awareness. And then sometimes His presence covers me with a mantle of serenity, and that's called the prayer of loving attention. Sometimes I only look at God and He looks at me. And that's the prayer of pure love.

And all that, my friend, is what dryness does. You see, the thing that for years you've thought was some terrible thing that happened to you was so wonderful.

What if you've prayed for a long, long time about something and you don't get an answer—how do you keep from despairing? You keep from despairing because that's your opportunity from God to exercise hope. Hope is the opposite of despair. When you despair, you see no good from what's happening to you. The fact that you've prayed a long time and don't seem to be getting what you want, it seems there's no good in that. But that's not true. Even if it lasts a long, long time, and you're convinced that God doesn't care, and there's no response, that's where God wants you to begin to exercise faith. Because faith says there *is* a response; it just happens to be *no* at this time.

God is automatically working in your soul. He is working in a very powerful way. But you don't see it. It's very easy to despair. But when we despair, we're really asking God to do something *we* want in the *way* we want it. This is where the prayer of humility comes in: "Lord, I trust that the fact that I am not getting what I feel I need at this moment, I trust that this is for my good, and I refuse to believe anything different." That's where your will comes in and makes a decision, and it keeps you from becoming resentful and despairing. You've prayed for something a long time, and it's a good thing you're praying for. But it's also a very good thing that you're being asked by God to exercise your will, to just say, "I love You, Lord, even when you say *no*." To exercise your faith. To see God in the present moment. To make you humble of heart: "Lord, I am before You as one who's helpless." So there's a tremendous amount of good that comes from having to wait a long time for an answer. That's what dryness does.

Now, how do you know the difference between being inattentive in prayer and just dozing off?

There is a prayer of quiet, where the soul is really raised to God. You can tell it afterward, when you wake up. Do you feel more virtuous? Do you feel you have rested in the Lord? Do you feel more serene? If you do, then the sleep you had may have been supernatural. If not ...

You see, God is Father. He doesn't love you less if you go to sleep. If you have a child, a very loving child, and he runs up and he wants to talk to you, and he's sitting on your lap and all of a sudden you look down and he's asleep, do you love him less? We shouldn't think that something I do makes God love me more. No, He just loves you all the time. Whether you're asleep or whether you're awake, when you sit and when you stand, He always loves you in the same infinite way.

The priest we had on the show last night said something that really touched my heart. He said that if you want to be healed of inner aches and pains, go sit before the Blessed Sacrament. Even if you fall asleep, the rays of that love heal you. Don't ever forget the tremendous power of just sitting in the presence of God.

* * *

Dryness can last a long time. I've been in dryness for forty years. That's a long time, but I wouldn't trade it at all. It took me years to understand. I used to fuss and fume and kick and scream. And then I realized that I must love God for Himself.

In a long period of dryness, there are moments of light, moments of joy and love, but they're very short, very fleeting. But what comes back is strong. We must praise God for dryness, because we can love God regardless of how we feel, no matter what.

Expectancy

Tonight our lesson will be on expectancy, which is the foundation for hope. Expectancy and hope go together like a hand in a glove. To see what we mean by *expectancy*, let's go back to when you're in your mother's womb, the expectancy of childhood.

Today, doctors tell us that a child in the womb knows when its mother is expectant, and when she wants the child or doesn't, when she is in pain or has had something terrible happen to her. God has put His breath into that child; He breathes the soul into the child, just as Jesus breathed upon the apostles and said, "Receive the Holy Spirit" (John 20:22). So God breathes a soul into that tiny, tiny, tiny embryo, where there is nothing but a heart beating. So that tiny child has a soul and it can sense, and it will go throughout nine months sensing that its mother loves it or doesn't love it. Some doctors will say you can talk to your baby, you can read to it. So there is an expectancy in that child, even though it is not aware of it intellectually; there is a sense. And as it grows into six months, seven months, eight months, nine months, there is an expectancy, and that child begins to move into position to be born.

And from the moment it's born, it is again expectant, for love, comfort, warmth, and food. And if it doesn't get any of these, or even one of these, it could be marked for life. It is expectant; it knows that every two or three hours during the night, although the parents are sound asleep, if it cries, something is going to happen. So there is a natural human expectancy that we have from our conception.

And then as the child grows, it becomes aware. It sees faces and hears voices, and there are some voices that it relates to much more readily than others, the voice of the mother and father. And it begins to say names; they may not be recognizable by anyone but the parents, but it begins to know. And this begins a life of expectancy, a real intellectual expectancy.

Now, if we are a Christian family, then all of this just comes together beautifully, and that child begins to grow in a very expectant way. It begins to trust. It trusts its parents, for example, because they are loving, and you trust those who are loving.

But today, with families being broken up—let's say, for example, if that child is not wanted and when it's born, it's not sure of love, it's not fed on time, it's not warm, it's not held in someone's arms, and so it feels very unloved. In a child like that, the expectancy level is very low. And you find a great difference in that child because it's not sure; it becomes aware of sadness, of misery. It might be abused, verbally, physically. I remember a woman with a little girl about four years old maybe, and she said to me right in front of the girl, "She was a mistake. I really didn't want her." I had to take a breath! I looked at that child, and she put her head down. And I said to the mother, "Aren't you ashamed to say that? How could you say that?" And I went to the child and told her, "God loves you."

I want you to know how important expectancy is, because it can either make or break you. Pray for your children. Don't wait until they're in trouble to pray for your children. Start praying for them when you know you're going to have a child. Pray for that child; pray for protection; pray for guidance; pray that that child always knows love. And when that child is in your womb, you want to consecrate that child to the Lord. You'll be surprised. That will heighten that child's expectancy, because it is already being raised to another level. Not only should you do that with the first child, but the second, the third, the fourth.

Now, it's really kind of exciting when you see a couple with their first child. They're so excited; every day they're telling you something new. The saddest thing is, when the second and the third or the fourth or fifth comes, they're not excited at all. Isn't it a shame how our expectancy level suddenly decreases? Every child is a gift. Every child is a wonder. Every child is something so special, and so you must look at your children as images — perfect, beautiful images of God. And treat them with love. And tell them you love them and they're God's gift to you.

You know, sometimes when you speak to your children, you can ruin their expectancy. We can say pretty belittling things, in jest. Your kid spills the water pitcher, and you say, "Why are you always so dopey?" That child might never forget that. Or you compare their grades. "This one made As. Why did you get Bs?" Well, he's a B student. Does that make him any less lovable? Or you say, "Well, I made As." Yes, but the child doesn't have your brains, and maybe that's a gift. You're a doctor, and you want your son to be a doctor, but maybe he wants to be a plumber. He might be the best plumber in the world. You've got to look at each one, because every time you look at them and try to mold them in the way God wants them to be molded, then you increase their expectancy. Why? Because they have hope. You see, the thing we destroy in each other so quickly is hope — when you let someone feel unloved, when you let them feel they're a big mistake, when you let them feel they're the dumbest of all your children, or they don't come up to someone else's level. And when those around them, their peers, keep doing the same thing, they lose expectancy. What is there to come?

Now we're going to look at teenagers and young adults. From the time a child is conceived and in all those years of growth, it begins to know God through the loving atmosphere of loving parents, or a loving parent. I say "parent" in the singular because I was brought up by my mother alone, and she was very loving to me. We had a lot of problems, a lot of tragedies, heartaches. But she loved me. So our experiences at this young age—although this isn't what happens today, but I'm talking about the goal, what the Lord wants, we need to know where we *should* be—if we've got that kind of loving awareness of love, we begin to know God, so that by the time you get to be a teenager, your experiences grow in faith, in wonder. And you begin to get inquisitive; you begin to say, "I wonder why you do this. I wonder why this is. And who made me? And why was I created?" So you begin to wonder.

It's at this point—even with all the questions and the doubts— it's at this point that our expectancy grows, because if you have a loving Father in Heaven, you begin to hope that one day you will see Him. That longing is a part of expectancy, to long for God. But what often happens today is that our teenagers are so beset with problems that stem from the early four, five, six years of life when they were unwanted, unloved, uncared for. So by the time they get to be teenagers in today's society, many of them are beset with adult problems, and they can't handle adult problems because they're not adults. They lack stability. They lack assurance because they have no assurance from their parents.

So I want to tell parents, you need to strive for stability in your family. Pray for the Lord to give you that spirit of expectancy, that even if things may be terribly depressing, you know it will be better. You know there is a purpose to this pain; there is a purpose to the suffering. It's that useless pain that kills us and destroys stability and assurance, when you don't know *why*. Sometimes you can just pat your child on the head or hug them or give them a word, just a plain word that says, "Hey, I know that things are rough. But let's stick together. It's gonna get better." The problem doesn't go away. Some problems can't; they take time. But what the child wants is not so much what's outside of him; what he wants so much is something inside that keeps him from getting sour, cynical, disheartened.

Our young people today are prime candidates for despair, and there is a tremendous amount of suicide today because they've lost expectancy. They've had rough childhoods, and they have a rough teenage life. They're always competing with their peers; they've been on dope, sex, the whole bit, so their minds are not developed yet; neither are their souls. So many of them live an adult life before they're able. Sometimes they just feel unloved for reasons of their own. It's not always a parent's fault. Sometimes society makes you feel unloved, or the tragedies that happen, or the weather that seems to destroy, the hurricanes and volcanoes. If you open a paper, you see things that make you feel not good enough, not lovable. All these things destroy that childlike joy that God wants us to have. No matter how miserable life is, He still wants us to have the joy, the joy that He promised that no one can take away from us.

You see, it's so important that we know that expectancy is something inside that carries us over and carries us through everything that could possibly happen to us — good, bad, or indifferent. When everything seems so urgent and everything is in a crisis, we have to realize that God transcends. God transcends everything around us. There's where our expectancy is. It is not in the things that pass; it is not in our misery; neither is it in our joy. It is in the Lord God, Who lives within me, Who loves me. If our youth could understand that one thing, then they would have that joy that the Lord promises us in John's Gospel.

Now, if we look at young adults — the expectancy of you young adults is so important, because you're the future leaders of this country, of this world. You're the future leaders in the Church. So expectancy gives us a joy, the joy of a new adventure, of a career that you're looking forward to, so that when you go to college, you have a definite goal in mind, and you ask the Lord: "Lord, tell me what it is You want me to do. What type of work can I do that will give You the greatest honor and glory?"

If you put God into everything in your life, you will have that expectancy. When you go to work early in the morning, you will have that expectancy of knowing that this is your day to love God, to love your neighbor. If you're Catholic and you've gone to Mass, or that's where you're headed, you have the expectancy of receiving the very Body and Blood, Soul and Divinity of the Lord. So we go with that kind of joy, knowing we're waiting. It's a joyful waiting. That's what expectancy is.

Then comes a time when you find someone you love, and you get married. What is marriage? Marriage is when two people love each other so much that their love becomes one love. And that one love must never lose its expectancy. When a young couple go on their honeymoon, we say, "Well, that won't last long." What do we mean by that? We mean that the expectancy will go. But it doesn't need to go. Because when the Lord blesses that couple with children, that is the concrete sign of your love; that's what the child is. Your love before seemed something ethereal, something almost out of this world. And yet, when you got married and you began to have children, an expectancy came along because love becomes a person.

Even though you may have problems or stress ... I don't think anybody ever got married who didn't have the stress of uncertainty:

"Am I gonna love this person forever? Am I gonna be able to take the faults and imperfections that I don't understand or I didn't see before?" When God begins to prune not only me but somebody I am living with, somebody I am sharing with, when I begin to see that everything I do concerns not just me but another person, and sometimes two or three, if I have a family ... If you've lost expectancy, then, all of a sudden, all of these things begin to crowd in on you, and the pruning and the sharing in difficult times becomes unbearable, because we lose sight of God bringing good out of everything. And what happens? We give up. "I'm not gonna take it anymore; I'm leaving." Because we don't have that expectancy that we are growing together. We are having difficult times, but we are growing. Our faults and weaknesses are not something that should tear us apart. They are something that should bring us together and make us more one, not make us turn away from each other. That happens with parents; that happens with children.

And so as you see, from conception to married life, we begin to realize that, unless God is that center ... And that includes people in single life; it includes single parents; it doesn't matter what your vocation is. You can be a hermit, a priest or religious, a married person, or someone just kind of floating around wondering what to do. It doesn't matter what your state is; we all must pray every day and say, "Lord, give me an expectant faith, an expectant faith that lives on the reality that God lives in us."

Let's talk now about the expectancy of middle age. There should be a kind of serenity beginning to flow in. If God has been the center of your life, throughout your rise and your fall (you're not always on an even keel), then as you begin your middle age, your love for your husband or wife should be more enduring, because it's not built so much on emotion; it is built on the will. You know each other; you know each other well. You're able to accept each other's faults, but you haven't lost expectancy. Your children are growing; your friends are more dear, old ones and new ones. All of it should increase your expectancy. You begin to have new freedoms, because as life has pruned and taken off rough spots, as you have suffered together and loved and born the heat of the day, as our Lord said, you begin to be molded together. And if you're trying to keep your family close-knit, then even though your children have problems, someone may run away, someone may leave, they come back. There's all this turmoil sometimes, but still, if you keep your expectancy high, saying, "The Lord God is with me; it's okay; we'll come out of this," then you begin to grow.

You see, expectancy is so attuned to hope. If I'm going to have faith that God is in the present moment, although I don't see Him, I don't feel Him, I know that everything is in the palm of His hand. That gives me faith. It takes away that human fear; it takes away that human element of despair and discouragement. So we are concerned but not worried. We're able to release things because we have that expectant faith, expectant hope. So if tragedies come along, and we certainly have had a terrible one today—those poor families of all of the servicemen coming home for Christmas. Suddenly over 260 men are killed when the plane exploded, while their loved ones are waiting at the airport. How can that kind of tragedy give you expectancy or hope? Well, you see, that's where faith comes in. It takes a lot of faith to keep on saying, "Lord, I expect, I hope, I love. And I'm sorry for those who do not love, do not hope, and do not believe in Thee."

When a tragedy like that just seems to crush you, till, like the Scripture says, you feel like you are in a wine press and there's not another drop of juice left; when you can raise your mind and heart to God and say, "Thy will be done," then your expectancy has grown in a most marvelous way. Because you have seen beyond, way beyond, the tragedy of today. The death of a loved one you know that you will never see in this life again. Sickness, when you see someone you love ill and there's nothing you can do. If you can put your mind and heart to say, "Lord, Thy will be done," and accept the pain and not run from it . . .

Some of you are out of work. There's nothing like having a family and rent to pay to make you so discouraged and so disheartened. But if your faith keeps on, and you keep looking for a job, and you keep trying to keep your family together, and they keep loving together, and they keep raising their mind and heart to God . . . Now, you might say, "Hey, wait a minute, that doesn't put food on the table." Yes, it does. Because discouragement and despair eat your heart right out of its place. So there is the need to always grow, regardless of our lifestyle. Well, sometimes our lifestyle takes our joy away—but regardless of our life condition.

So when we get to old age . . . I went to the restaurant the other day, and I looked at the menu, and the same hamburger that somebody else had to pay full price for, those over fifty-five could get for $2.50. So I realized I was over the hill. And being over the hill, I just ordered a hamburger, thinking my gray hair would make it obvious and she'd give it to me for $2.50, but she didn't. I paid four bucks. I should have been flattered. There is the expectancy of old age, but sometimes today, there isn't any. There should be. There should be the joy of grandchildren. You see, from you and your husband or your wife came all of these people, to people the kingdom with new interest and new lives and new talents.

So it's a time for spiritual renewal. It's not a time for depression. It's not a time to look and say, "This is what I used to do. I can no longer do this; I can no longer do that." You see, expectancy makes you accept your age. Some people will never tell their age. I'm sixty-two. I don't mind. I don't think it matters. Because you see, I'm on the way. I've spent my life on my journey; it's like what St. Paul says, "I am far from thinking that I have already won [but] … I strain ahead for what is still to come" (Phil. 3:12-13). He is still running. This is a man who has expectancy. He's got that force to keep going. He says here, "I forget the past." Oh, if we could all forget the past! "I forget the past and I strain ahead for what is still to come; I am racing for the finish" (3:13-14).

You all know what that is in a human way. You save for a year and a half to buy a car. You're all expectancy, and you go and look at it. But after you've got it, well, the expectancy dies off, and it's just another car. And you expect something else; you hope for something else. Whatever you have, expectancy comes and goes.

But with supernatural expectancy, it just keeps on growing. It's not a kind of yo-yo up and down thing. It keeps growing. Your love now is so much more pure than it was before. Now you love your partner, you love your children, with a much deeper love, because there has been enough pain mixed with it to make it more secure. And a part of expectancy is security. You have more hope, because you've lived through tragedies, you've lived through pain, so now you're not afraid of it anymore. You're not running from anything or anyone, and as a result, you don't lose your expectancy of what is to come. Your prayer is so much deeper; your prayer life is so much deeper. Before, you used to just ask God for things; you prayed vocally, mentally, whatever way you prayed. But now, you can just sit down and talk to God heart-to-heart. So your prayer is an expectant prayer. Whether you kneel to pray or sit to pray, you're there, and you know that God is with you. You have an expectant love and expectant prayer.

When two people are in love and they are willing to unite with each other, the whole plan is that their love can express itself freely, and they cannot in any way then take away a possibility of new life coming from that love. Sometimes we have perhaps lost the sense of what love is all about. When the Father and the Son love each other, the fruit is the Spirit. Our problem is our own selfishness, to say, "I don't want the child." Why do we not want the child? Maybe we can't afford any more children. The Church has allowed natural family planning as an alternative. It takes sacrifice, but at least it doesn't take away God's plan in allowing married couples to be part of His creative life.

Even if a child is abused, abuse has nothing to do with his being born; it has to do with the attitude of his parents. You can't keep throwing out the baby with the dirty water. You see, if I have a choice of killing somebody, robbing them, or annihilating them by slander, I can't say one of them is a lesser evil. I can lose my soul over any one of those, so there is no such thing as lesser evil. And although a child may be abused … I had a hard childhood, and there were times when I just wondered if anybody loved me, including God. But I thank God for it all—for giving me the chance to live, the chance to know Him, the chance to serve Him. What we're saying is that the abused child of today is going to be useless tomorrow. I'm sure that's true in some cases, but I know in many cases, it has made men strong. You see, we've got to eradicate the abuse and not eradicate the people. We've got to instill in our hearts compassion and love and understanding for each other. And only our union with God can bring us all together again in concern for one another.

Well, I think what we need to understand is we have lost the concept of the beauty of a child, the image of God and the love within it. The reason for that is that we are always and forever looking at what we can give them. In other words, if I want to give my children everything, and my everything can exist only for two children. But what is everything? The things that the children need today, if you talk to any of them, the most abused, the thing they wanted—they would be willing to have one slice of bread rather than three, and they'd be willing to have peanut butter for Christmas, if they were loved. So when we're saying we don't want children because we don't have enough to give them, give the child love, and you'll be surprised. I used to go hungry day after day when I was a kid. I know you can be hungry and you can be thirsty and you can be lonely, if you love. Because love fulfills and gives you the courage to carry on. And one day, that abused child that we wish had never been born will see the face of God. And when you see that abused child, you will see the most beautiful creature in this world. You will be awestruck by the beauty of that child who was so abused. Because God is just and God will make that child something of wonder in the kingdom.

Every person who has been created has always been in the mind of God. Before time began, you and I were in the mind of God. Now, whether or not your children make the right choices that will enable them to accept God fully to their death, or at least at their death ... When we talk about salvation, we're talking about personal choices. But you consecrated them to the Lord, and that's what's so beautiful. If you consecrate your children to the Lord, or even if you haven't done it at birth, do it now, especially those of you who might be having problems. Tonight, before you go to bed, say, "Lord, I give You my children; I give You my loved ones." And you can have that expectancy that the Lord honors that and will take care of them. Put your children and put your loved ones in His hands. You may not live to see them be transformed as you would like them to be transformed. It doesn't matter. You know that you can have an assured expectancy that God will take care of them, and you will see them again in His kingdom, because you can trust Him.

Imploring God's Mercy on This World

Today, if you look at the news, if you look at the world, it seems to be going down, down, down, down, down, down, down. It can be frightening. There are so many unknowns. I think it is a kind of sad, joyous thing. We just want God to get honor and glory. I feel that the time is rapidly coming upon us when the Lord God is going to show Himself in many different ways—personal, communal, national, international. Because God's love demands His justice.

Our concept of justice is very severe, and so when I punish somebody it's really with a kind of vengeance. But God doesn't do that. Every time God punishes, it's out of love. And that's important to understand. So many times when we correct, it is not out of love. We just dislike the person who has done something wrong, and so we get very personally upset. We make that person think that we're angry with him instead of angry with what he does or did. God, on the other hand, cannot correct you—no matter how harsh it seems—He cannot correct you except out of love. He does it to bring you back.

You and I know, my friends, that so many of us never really go back to God until we're in a lot of trouble. We just don't think of God. It's as if we say to the Lord, "Look, I'll handle this as long as everything is okay. When things go bad, then You can come into my life. Otherwise, You stay up there in your nice comfortable Heaven, and I will stay here on my comfortable earth. When I'm in need, I'll call You."

And so what I'm asking you to do tonight is to strengthen yourself in prayer and sacrifice as you've never done before. *Pray.* So many of you are lonely in apartment houses. So many of you have children perhaps who never come to see you. So many of you are sick with terminal diseases, cancer, whatever it might be, lonely in convalescent homes, in prisons. Wherever you are, whatever pain you have, whatever suffering it is, give it to God like incense before the throne.

I guess what I'm asking you to do is to pray as you've never prayed before. You know, in the book of Samuel, it says it is a sin not to pray (1 Sam. 12:23). I want you to understand that, today, prayer is more important than your food on your table. I'm asking you to gather together as a family. I don't care how disruptive your family is. I don't care how angry you are with each other. I don't care if husband and wife have been quarreling. Get together just once—once a day, once a week—and kneel down in the name of Jesus, in the name of the Eternal Father, and say, "God, Lord, we have sinned against You." I don't think there's any one of us who couldn't say with the prodigal son, "God, Father, I have sinned against Heaven and earth. I have sinned against You and men. Have mercy on me." I want you to get together as a family, as a community, as a prayer group. If you're by yourself, if you're single in an apartment, kneel down with God Himself, Who is ever present in your midst, and with your guardian angel pray for the world. Pray for the world.

You know, if you want to plant a seed, you've got to prepare the ground. It just isn't going to grow on a rock. You've got to prepare the ground, and the ground that you prepare will make that particular bush or shrub or tree grow. The ground that you are preparing when you pray is love. Did you ever wonder why some of your prayers are not answered, besides the fact that it may not be the will of God? Some of our prayers are not answered because we do not love. And we condemn our brother. What does it mean, to condemn? To condemn means I look at you and I judge your motive, and then I push you aside as unworthy of my love. First of all, I cannot get into a person's mind and judge. I can judge his actions. But we don't know motives. So what I'm saying to you is that the ground, the ground for answered prayer, is love and compassion.

Jesus came as man; He lived, He died, He suffered, and He rose. With all of that, mankind still has a hard time believing in a God. We may no longer understand what it meant for a God to come down because we don't know God. If we knew God, we would stand in awe at the fact that He would come down as a child, come down and be spit upon and slapped in the face. But we're so busy about so many things. We're so busy with sin and pleasure, hatred and revenge. I think when we pray, my friends, we need to pray to the Father and ask for forgiveness because we so little appreciate His gift, the gift of His Son.

What would happen if someone on Christmas morning gave you a great gift: a beautiful mansion and a great big Rolls-Royce. These are material things, but it draws a picture. And if he said, "This is a gift for you. Merry Christmas!" and you looked at it and shrugged and then, to add insult to injury, you went and lived across the street in a *shack*—and, worst of all, you *liked* it in the shack—we would say, "Oh, such ingratitude." Oh, my friends, that is nothing compared with what we have done to the almighty majestic God in our midst. We have said to God today, "I will not serve." We say it in all kinds of ways. By indifference, lukewarmness, a habit of sin. "God doesn't care," we say. "I'm not hurting anybody." How can you say that? The first one you hurt is yourself when your soul shrivels up like a prune.

We offend the Father so much by ingratitude for His gift of Jesus and of His Son's Mother, Mary. It just makes my heart ache when I see so many people putting so much money and time and labor into such terrible literature against Our Lady, against the Church, against the pope. Don't you have anything else to do? Is your whole life geared toward destruction? Read the Bible, especially that part that says, "Love one another. And do not condemn." How do we think we're going to face God?

Those of you who understand what I'm saying, pray to Mary. When you pray to Mary, you pray to Jesus. You pray for each other. I hope you pray for me. I pray for you. Every creature God made, especially this one woman, Mary, is so fantastic. We honor God when we honor any of His creatures, and especially this one, nature's solitary boast. I think we need to ask her to intercede for us, to ask Mary, the Mother of God, to ask her Son to have mercy on all mankind, because I believe the time of accounting is coming.

You and I must be concerned about the salvation of souls, about their welfare, not only our own. Not only your own soul, but the whole world. You can't look at a news program, you can't open a magazine or a newspaper, without looking at wars and the most terrible atrocities. And you know the sad thing to me? It's just *news*. People are murdered in airports, in fields, and cities, every day. Every day we see buildings torn apart and children lying dead, and it's just news. Do you ever cry? Do you ever cry over those who starve, those who are cold?

I read a magazine not too long ago, from a certain city in our country, talking about those who live in the streets and how they pushed them out into the dumps. And one of the dignitaries of that city was asked, "Why do you do that? How can you do that?" And he said, "Well, that's what you have to do with those who do not produce." We're regressing to the survival of the fittest.

I read another article on euthanasia. If we can kill them before they got a chance to be born, then certainly we're going to kill them when they get old. I mean, this person is suffering. Is it not an act of charity? Let me tell you, my friends, and whoever listens to my voice this night: the Lord God Almighty is Sovereign Lord. He is Lord of Life, and He is Lord of death. He decides who lives. And He decides who dies. No one has a right to make that decision.

You may say it's painful, and it is. You may say often it is too much, and it may be. You may say, "Lord, how long?" when time seems endless. But He alone has the right to say, "Come." And you see, we often don't even have the conscience that there's something wrong here. We don't seem to comprehend the awesomeness of the sin of murder. We've somehow gotten so far from God. And so I ask you in your prayer to pray for conversion, a change of life, a change of mind, a change of heart. We need to recognize our sins, and we need to pray for those who do such violent acts against society. We need to pray for the victims of those acts. We need to have a heart of flesh. We are becoming a people stiff-necked and with a heart of stone. We need to recognize our sins. We need to stand before God and say, "God, Lord of all, give me an understanding of my sins. Show me what I am. Even though I tremble before Thee in fear, Jesus gives me hope and joy."

One day, my friends, you and I will stand before God, either in this life or the next, and our sins will accuse us. I am a sinner, and you are; we're all sinners. It's the acknowledgment that so often is not there. I think if the Father were to come down, I think He would look at us and He would say, "The sacrifice of my Son is in some places laughed at and in other places little regarded." He would say, "In the Old Testament, I was hard on you. And you were full of fear, and you strayed away from me. And so I gave you a New Testament. And in the New Testament, I give you love. And I thought love would draw you to me. I thought, especially if I gave you my most precious Son, I thought I would reach you so quickly. But after two thousand years, you have grown cold and have forgotten my love and my Son."

My friends, I think we need in our prayers to pray for God's mercy because hope comes to those who will offer themselves and make sacrifices to the Lord. The Lord has never held anything back from you. There is absolutely nothing that the Lord could have possibly done that He has not done for you. You say, "I don't have material riches; I'm very poor." But you are rich in spirit. That's what's important.

We've gotten to a place today where we're ashamed to talk about God. You know, there's a trite little saying that one never talks about God and politics. You speak about politics. But you're ashamed to speak about God. You're ashamed. You'll laugh at a dirty joke, and tell one even worse, because you don't want to be considered "holier than thou." Why are you afraid to speak about Jesus to others? You know, in the Church, we've got a lot of people that we call saints. And a lot of people on earth, wonderful holy Christians, who will speak out and talk about Jesus. You say, "They turn me off." Okay, maybe they are a little strong; maybe they are a little bit overboard. That doesn't excuse you, though, from mentioning His name in a loving way instead of using it as a swear word. What is it when you swear? Does it make you feel more manly? To offend God and take His name in vain makes you feel strong? No, you're weak, because you don't have the willpower to speak His name with respect. You're afraid. People have lived and died for the name of Jesus.

We get so involved in things and people and worries. That's what Our Lord says chokes the word. The power in Heaven that's yours and mine is sometimes forgotten and very, very little used. You, as a Christian, have great power in the kingdom. The Father waits for souls to dedicate and consecrate themselves to His honor and glory. You youth out there listening to me tonight, you have a lot of potential. Go out and preach the good news that Jesus is Lord. But before you open your mouth, at least make the effort to live what you preach.

As the Lord visits us in various ways, some painful, some not, He does so to teach His wisdom, so we know that God does not bow down before men. That's what we're asking Him to do. So many ask God to bow down before men. We want to make all the decisions that are God's prerogative, God's right. We hear so much today about rights, but I never hear anything about God's rights. I think that if God were to come again, He would have to reprimand us and remind us that He does not bow before men. He would look at you and He would look at me, and He would say, "You must stand in awe of my greatness."

Every day, I pray that Jesus comes and saves us. He already saved us, I know. But do *you* know? How many people out there know? I want you to thirst for God and not for the things of this world. You live in them, and you've got to use them. We're human beings, not angels, and we've got to work and sleep and recreate. We live and we die; we marry and we bury. But in the heart, there must be constant growth because God is the only one Who can fill your heart and soul with good things. All of you who have reached fifty or sixty years old—and unfortunately, today, some of our youth have already reached that stage where they "know." They've tried everything before their time, and they're miserable. That's why there's so many young people who commit suicide—after you've done it all and you don't have God, that's a big fat zero. There's nothing standing in front of you. God is the only source that can fill you with love and everlasting joy and everlasting peace.

You and I have one life to live, and it's extremely short. Did you ever notice that if somebody says, "My mother is very ill," the first thing you ask is, "How old is she?" I don't know what difference that makes. How old is she? She's seventy-five. So we consider her on the way out. But the soul is not old. The soul isn't wrinkled; the soul is not gray-haired; the soul is not tired. The soul is youthful and everlasting and immortal. I'm sixty-two. I get a little creaky here and there; it's harder to get out of bed. You get a little stiff, and your legs don't move as fast. You get more tired, more out of breath, whatever. But every moment of life, I have the opportunity of saying yes to God, be it ever so difficult, ever so tragic, ever so painful. I have an opportunity of saying, "Lord, this is my gift to You: my misery, my sins, my weaknesses, my mistakes. The good I've done. The good You've done in me. I give it to You."

There are so many people who live in confusion today. Adultery is a man's privilege. Or a woman's privilege, sometimes. Homosexuality, abortion, euthanasia. All these things say, "I will not serve." Pride is an awesome thing. We all have it. And then there's a certain form of humanism that says, "As long as you're doing good, the end justifies the means."

And hatred. The hatred is unbelievable. You see nation fighting against nation, and it's the poor, the innocent, who suffer so much. And then from war comes a nation of vengeance: "You do this to me, and I'm gonna do that to you." And it just keeps going on and on, like a terrible monster that gets bigger and bigger and bigger and bigger. Hatred breeds more hatred. Vengeance breeds more hatred. To most of us Americans, who have been so blessed by God to never have a bomb on our shores, it's just news. Just news. I want you to think of what I've said. I want you to examine your conscience and say, "Oh God, tell me tonight, how do I stand before You?" And don't just pray for yourself; pray for your family and pray for mankind. Everyone is your brother. And you are your brother's keeper. Let us acknowledge our sins. Say, "Lord, I have sinned against You."

I would suggest something that the sisters do every day—two things. Implore the mercy of God through a little chaplet called the Chaplet of Divine Mercy. Even if in your family you don't pray together and you are all angry with each other, do it, because this world, my friends (and you're in it), the world is in a lot of trouble. Please, say the Chaplet every day. This is something we're going to begin on the Network, the *Catholic devotional hour*. The Rosary and the Chaplet every night, so you as a family can pray it with us. I don't care whether you're Catholic, Methodist, Jehovah's Witness. I don't care what you are, please, implore the mercy of God. If you don't want to use this Chaplet, just get on your knees and say it in your own words.

The Rosary, too, is very necessary. It begins with a Credo, an Our Father, the Hail Mary. Say it every day. You don't have time? Cancel one of your soap operas. Your soap opera is not doing you any good. But *this* will—the Mother of God and Divine Mercy. I'm not pushing my devotions on you. I'm just being practical and logical and looking at the signs of the times. Don't push these signs under a bushel. They are not going to go away.

I'm going to start speaking more about the evils in the world. I hope these lessons shake you up. Why? Although we do talk about love and Jesus and joy and miracles and all the rest, my friends, there's a negative aspect of life. It's getting darker and bleaker and blacker every minute. And that is sin. War, crises, vengeance, resentment, anger, lust, and all of those things. People are afraid to walk the streets. These are signs of the times.

And I'm going to start speaking a lot about God's sovereign rights. Because He loves you so much. Don't hurt Him. He's given you everything. What do you want? What do you want from God? What more do you want? We have a lot of false gods today. Pleasure, sex, alcohol, drugs. Good times, whatever that is. Wealth, ambition, lust, glory, pride. I think we need to speak more about how God's justice is a part of His mercy. If I saw you running and I knew there was a terrible precipice there, and I would have to jump on you and drag you back and skin your knees, although you were hurting, it would be a justice that was merciful.

And then my friends, there's one other thing I want you to do, those of you that are Catholic. Please make an effort to go to Mass every day if you can. If you can't, do the best you can. The Eucharist, the mercy of God, and Mary. Three things I'm asking you to do.

And I want to just say a little bit about the litany of the Divine Mercy. I'm just going to read some parts of it to you so we can end this program in prayer.

> Divine Mercy, gushing forth from the bosom of the
>   Father, I trust in You.
> Divine Mercy, incomprehensible mystery, I trust in You.
> Divine Mercy, unfathomed by any intellect, human or
>   angelic, I trust in You.
> Divine Mercy, better than the heavens, I trust in You.
> Divine Mercy, encompassing the whole universe,
>   I trust in You.
> Divine Mercy, descending to earth in the Person of Jesus,
>   I trust in You.

Divine Mercy, enclosed in the Heart of Jesus, flowing
out of His wound and His heart, I trust in You.
Divine Mercy, accompanying us through our whole life,
I trust in You.
Divine Mercy, embracing us especially at the hour of
death, I trust in You.
Divine Mercy, shielding us from the fire of Hell,
I trust in You.
Divine Mercy, who astonish angels and are incomprehensible to saints, I trust in You.
Divine Mercy, unfathomed in all the mysteries of God,
I trust in You.
Divine Mercy, lifting us out of every misery,
I trust in You.
Divine Mercy, source of our happiness and joy,
I trust in You.
Divine Mercy, in which we are all immersed,
I trust in You.
Divine Mercy, sweet relief for anguished hearts,
I trust in You.
Divine Mercy, only hope of despairing souls—don't
take your life, my friend; trust His mercy to pull you
through this sorrow, this pain; let Him be Sovereign
Lord of your life—I trust in You.
Divine Mercy, repose of hearts, peace in the midst
of all our fears, I trust in You.
Divine Mercy, inspiring hope against all hope,
I trust in You.

That's a great way to go to bed. To trust in the mercy of the
Father, who gave so much and asks so little. He doesn't ask you all

to be monks and nuns. He wants you to be faithful to your state in life, and He wants you to be joyful and have happy days. He wants you to work and have a family, but He wants you to have Himself, without which there is no happiness, there is no joy. You can't get happiness out of a bottle; all you get is a headache. You can't get happiness out of lust because all you do is destroy your body. You can't get happiness out of extravagance because there comes a time when you're nauseated at having too much. You can't get it out of money because it's nothing but paper. The stock market went down so far that some lost thousands, millions, in only twenty-four hours. So we find happiness only in God. That's it. All these other things, the Lord says, will be added to you, but it's sounding brass and ashes without God. I hate to tell you, but you're on a merry-go-round. You're running. But you're not going anywhere.

You and I don't need to be afraid if the Lord comes, or if His love decides to correct us harshly, if we've prayed and loved much and were Jesus to our neighbor and implored His mercy.

I wish you Heaven. I wish you life. I wish you God. I wish you Jesus. I ask that your night be blessed. I ask that your days be filled with hope. I ask that you are humble enough to admit your faults, and that includes myself. And let us pray. If we are going to be full of fear in any way, let us fear the One who has the power to throw both body and soul into Hell. That One we fear. The ones who can kill you, you have no need to fear. I love you. I wish you God's blessing, His love, His peace, and His joy. And let us pray for each other that we will all be the recipients of His marvelous mercy.

The Mysteries of the Rosary

Tonight, we will be introducing you to the mysteries of the Rosary. For those of you who really don't know what in the world we're doing when we pray the Rosary, I'm going to show you. It's very, very simple, and it's a prayer designed to keep the mind from wandering.

So you begin with this crucifix, praying the Credo: "I believe in God, the Father Almighty ..."

Then you have five beads: an Our Father, three Hail Marys, and another Our Father. The three Hail Marys are for faith, for hope, and for love.

What in the world is a Hail Mary? The first part comes from St. Luke's Gospel, beginning with chapter 1, verse 28: *Hail Mary, full of grace. The Lord is with you. Blessed are you among women. Blessed is the fruit of your womb* (1:42). And we add the name *Jesus*. And then we say a prayer that has been added through the centuries: *Holy Mary, Mother of God*—which is stated in St. Luke's Gospel—*pray for us*—because that's her role, she is the intercessor of all intercessors, so we ask her to pray for us—*now,* at this moment, *and at* that most important moment of our life, *the hour of our death.*

Now, in order to keep our minds on the life of Jesus—that's the whole essence of Christianity, to live out the life of Jesus. Everyone lives the life of Jesus. We all have our joys; we all have our sorrows; and we all have those moments, be they ever so short, that are glorious. So we begin then with what we call the *Joyful Mysteries*—because they are joyful. However, I always considered them kind of bittersweet. That's the way life is most of the time. There are tragedies and heartaches, frustrations, but then there are moments that are joyful. Bittersweet. And what are the Joyful Mysteries?

First, the *Annunciation*. That's in St. Luke's Gospel, when the Angel Gabriel announces to Mary the wonder of wonders, that the Word would be made flesh and dwell in our midst. He would have the same bone as I have, the same flesh, the same blood. And as your body was formed in the womb of your mother, blood of her blood, with a soul breathed into it by God, so the Eternal Word, who was forever with the Father, came down into the womb of Mary—that's why we love her so much—and began the process of growth.

Then, again in St. Luke's Gospel, the *Visitation*. Mary visits her cousin Elizabeth, and in that beautiful encounter, we find the whole essence of when does life begin. When does life begin? It says here that our Lady went with haste, meaning quickly, to her cousin Elizabeth, who was already six months pregnant with St. John. Now, just think. It means that in this mystery alone, the Lord God tells us when life begins. Because within the womb of Mary, the Incarnate Word was just conceived through the Holy Spirit, and she *hastens* to Elizabeth. No matter how long it took her, the Lord couldn't have been more than a week or so old by the time she arrived. But what does Elizabeth say at this visitation? She says, "Who am I that the mother of my Lord should come to me?" She solved the problem. We're running around with doctors and physicians trying to figure out when does life begin, and it's right here. Because Elizabeth called Mary "mother," "mother of my Lord," already. And that is when John was sanctified in his mother's womb. She said, "The child in my womb leapt for joy." That was the purpose of Mary visiting Elizabeth.

And that's what you think about, you see. The Rosary is just not a rattling prayer. It's a prayer that makes you bring to your mind the Gospel. It's something you do and say so that your mind can meditate, think, about the whole essence of life. And why do I say bittersweet? Well, as joyful as the Annunciation is and the Visitation, there must have been in the mind of Mary: "How do I tell Joseph?" There was in the background this cross.

Then we come to the *Nativity*, the birth of Jesus. Bittersweet again. I can imagine Mary making little clothes and Joseph making a rocking crib. And everything suddenly was gone. I'm sure they thought they had enough time to go to Bethlehem and come back to Nazareth. It never happened. The Child was born in a smelly cave. Not the nice clean thing that you have at Christmas. There are animals in there. We've got animals, so we know. So there was the beauty of birth, giving birth to the Son of the Most High God, but in a cold, wet cave. No one there to sing *Alleluia* until the shepherds came, until the wise men came. And there was Joseph with his terrible heartache of knowing that his wife was chosen by God among all women, so blessed to bear the Messiah, and what was he able to give Him? Nothing better than a cave. So the joy of the Nativity was mixed. It had to be, because they were loving people.

Then we come after that to the *Presentation in the Temple*. When Mary and Joseph went up to the temple, they were very poor. They didn't have a sheep or a goat to offer, so they have a few turtledoves worth a few pennies. They brought the turtledoves, and then Simeon comes, the old, old man, and Anna. They've been waiting and praying and praying so hard for the Messiah, and suddenly, they watch this young couple coming up with a child in their arms, and Simeon knows. And he says, "Now, Master, You can let Your servant go in peace." He was ready to die. "Because my eyes have seen the salvation which You have prepared for us."

Then Jesus grows to about twelve, and we see Him going to Jerusalem for the holidays. Suddenly, Joseph thinks He's with Mary, and Mary thinks He's with Joseph. And they come to that place where they stop overnight, and Joseph says to Mary, "Where is Jesus?" She says, "I thought He was with you." And he says, "No, I thought He was with you." And there comes a terrible fear: "What happened to my Son?" We find then another joyful mystery, the *Finding of Jesus in the Temple*. These are the Joyful Mysteries, because they all had tremendous joy. But all of them, bittersweet.

And then come the *Sorrowful Mysteries*. All of them in the Scriptures. The whole Rosary is in the Scriptures. So the idea again is to bring our mind back to the reality of how much God loves you. How much He loves me. And so we find the *Agony in the Garden*. When you and I find it hard to accomplish the will of God, we have only to say that mystery to know it was also hard for Jesus. "Not my will, but Your will be done." That's the Agony in the Garden.

The second Sorrowful Mystery is the *Scourging at the Pillar*. They tie Our Lord to a post and make Him hang taut so that His skin is very, very stretched. And according to the Shroud of Turin, there were six different people who whipped Him with metal slugs, leather tongs. So bruised, Scripture says, that He hardly looked like a man.

Then, to mock Him, they crowned Him with thorns, to mock His kingship. When you are so distraught, mentally distraught, when you have a problem with your pride, when you're so broken-hearted over someone who left you, or when someone who loved you no longer loves you, think of these mysteries. Think of the *Crowning with Thorns*. Say these mysteries; that's what they're for: to know that Jesus went through the same thing, only a million times multiplied in intensity of pain. The Rosary is not a devotion so much as a living Gospel.

And then *Jesus carries His Cross*. The agony of putting wood on a back that was already scourged, already beaten, already bleeding, already sore. And if you've ever made the Stations of the Cross, you know the pain, you know the degree of love, and every one of these mysteries, especially when He dies, the *Crucifixion*, every single one of these mysteries says how much Jesus loves you. How very, very much He loves you.

You know? Sometimes our cross seems so heavy. And it is. Sometimes our situation seems so hopeless. And it is. Sometimes it seems like everybody is against us. And maybe they are. And so, on a human level, you find no comfort and no consolation. And you're right. But unless you look at the Cross of Jesus, there is no rhyme or reason to the pain in your life. Unless you can put your life beside His and get courage and strength from that life, you see, nothing makes any sense.

And that's why He came. It's the mystery of mysteries. I may love you; I may pray for you or wish you well; and I may do all the things that would make you happy. But am I willing to take on your burden? Am I willing to take on your pain, just to feel how you feel? It's hard to say. You see, the reason the Messiah came as a Suffering Servant is because that is the most exquisite way of saying, "I love you." You never have to wonder about it. You never have to question His love. No matter how low you fall, He is always ready, because He did all of this for your love.

When we pray the Rosary, it's a mini Scripture. It gives us the opportunity and kind of forces the mind to think about one aspect of the large life, so you can equate it with your life at the present moment. So we've gone over the Joyful Mysteries and seen how they were bittersweet, very much like life is. There's a joy in it, but then, all of a sudden, there is a fear; there's a trial somewhere hidden within it. Then there are the tragedies in your life or those heartaches, when it just seems so deep that there seems to be no silver lining in the future.

And then come those moments in life that are glorious. So we look at the first *Glorious Mystery:* the *Resurrection of Jesus.* And you and I have our resurrections. There are times when you and I struggle and fight and work on a particular virtue or weakness we want to overcome, and suddenly one day we find we have overcome; we are getting better. It's a resurrection. It's a new life. And those of you that have become what we call today "newborn." You were born again in the Spirit. You begin to know, to understand, that there is a God and that God loves you. Something, everything, begins to fall into place, and that's a kind of resurrection. But Jesus had a real Resurrection. And you and I will have a real resurrection. One day you and I, this very body, will rise again, but glorious. Different. The same but different. I can be the same but different. If you look at a picture of me twenty years ago, I'd be the same person, but I'd look different today than I did twenty years ago. When we rise again, when our soul is reunited to our body, we will be different, but the same person. And this is what you want to think of when things get very, very bad for you, when everything seems lost. Look forward, look forward to your resurrection.

Then is the *Ascension of Our Lord.* You can find it in the Gospel. The Rosary is very, very Gospel-oriented. People say Catholics never read the Gospel. That's ridiculous. All the Masses: the Gospel. All of the Offices: Scripture or the Gospel. And the Rosary, again, the Gospel. So now, when Our Lord ascended into Heaven, He brought with Him many. Did you ever realize that? We're going to come back to that in a minute, when we go to the mystery of the Assumption.

Then came *Pentecost*, when the Holy Spirit came down upon us, and we all know what that means. Jesus promised; He said, "If I go, I will send the Advocate, the Sanctifier." He is the one that is with you today. It is the Spirit that fills you with the love of Jesus, fills you with the determination to be like Jesus. That's what this Rosary is all about; it's a constant reminder of the life of Jesus parallel to your own life. And so you have moments, like at your Confirmation, when the Spirit came upon you and renewed His seven gifts: made you strong, loving, understanding, with more wisdom, with more counsel, with more strength and fortitude and piety. All of these things He gave you and renewed, and He renews them every day, every day in your soul, so you grow in faith and hope and love. And that's what the Holy Spirit does. He's the one that makes you holy, as God is holy.

Then comes the *Assumption*. Now, some of you will say, "I don't buy that." It's logical, since Mary is conceived without sin through the merits of her Son. She benefited by the merits of redemption before it happened, so that she could be this peerless creature, this inviolate temple, this holy of holies for the Son of God to come into and become man. Had Adam and Eve not sinned, there would be no death. So Mary was created and conceived without sin for the purpose of being that special vehicle of the Incarnate Word. For that reason alone, she benefited by the merits of redemption ahead of time. So, it's logical that just as you and I would have never died, had Adam and Eve not sinned—when it was time to go to Heaven, the Lord would have taken us up, but since they sinned, we are doomed to die—because Mary was without that sin, there was no reason for her not to rise and be assumed into

Heaven. Some of you don't believe that. Well, now you answer me a question: What happened to the people who rose from the grave when Jesus died (Matt. 27:52–53)? Do you think they went back down into the grave? I don't think so. I think they were His triumph when He ascended into Heaven. It's not common, that's true. But the Scriptures do give us a few examples of people assumed into Heaven: Enoch. Elijah.

Now we come to the *Coronation*. Our Lady was crowned as Queen of Heaven and Earth. You can read it in the book of Revelation. Even just pure logic tells you that if Jesus is king, His Mother is queen. You can't just use her and then push her aside. You're talking about the Mother of God.

Well, we've gone through the Glorious Mysteries. I want you now to get out your rosary. I hope that it brings within your heart a spirit of prayer and reverence and awe. So let us pray the Rosary. The important thing about it is that you see the depiction of the particular mystery that you're saying, and that your mind and your heart are raised up to God. We hope that the mysteries of the Rosary will enhance your spiritual life, your walk with God, because it brings Jesus very near. It gives us the reality of how much He loved us. You never know how much someone loves you until things get really bad. The friend, the loved one, who sticks with you when things are difficult is the one that loves you most. In fact, you judge, you will judge someone's deep love by how they act toward you when you're in a crisis, when there's a tragedy, when you're at fault or you're guilty of something, or you have fallen deeply sad. That person stuck with me to the end. That person knows me. That's exactly what Jesus did. He did it for you, and He did it for me.

The mysteries of the Rosary, as I said before, are a mini Scripture. They bring your mind to Jesus in the midst of these mysteries. The Spirit will bring mysteries and understanding to your mind that you've never had before. You begin to understand Jesus and His Mother. You begin to understand why Jesus suffered so much for love of you. We can understand the Joyful Mysteries and how they apply to our daily life. It's not something in the past. The mysteries of the Rosary are something *now*, something present, because you live them. There are days you're joyful; there are days you're sorrowful; there are days that are glorious in your life. And in each one of these aspects of your daily life, Jesus must be a part. You must know that He went through the same thing to a higher degree.

And so the Rosary is an opportunity to say to God, "I give you fifteen minutes of my day." To say, "I love You." To say, "I'm grateful." To say, "I thank You, Lord, for every pain. For every joy. For every sorrow." To say, "I thank you, Mary, for following Jesus no matter what, from His conception, to His death, to His Resurrection, to His Ascension, to Pentecost, and up to the moment when the Lord said, 'Come.'" At that moment she rose, as you and I will rise one day, and sits with her Son in the glory of the kingdom. She is there as your intercessor; she is there to love you, to pray for you, to intercede for you, to protect you, to guard you, to send you grace upon grace. And to let you know that she's the Mother of all mothers, the friend of all friends, the companion of all companions. She understands; she is loving and patient; she's compassionate, a source of solace when we're in pain. She's help of Christians and queen of martyrs. She's everything you and I want to be. She's that perfect disciple — the one who never said *no* to God. May you and I one day meet her face-to-face and thank her for her sacrifices. As we see her Son so glorious in His kingdom, when He says to you and to me as He said to her, "Come, enjoy the fruits of your pain, your suffering."

Part 2

KEYS TO THE SPIRITUAL LIFE

Trusting God in the Present Moment

I've been talking with the sisters now for quite a while about St. John's Gospel, chapters 14-17, and I noticed as we were talking together, the sisters and I, that this particular section of the Gospel of John is the farewell address. You know, if you knew you were going to die in a day or two and you wanted to leave your family something very important, then you would measure your words, you would be very careful what you said, and you would get in the most important things, because you don't have time for superfluities. So the Lord in this farewell address gave us, so to say, the whole rule of leading a Christian life, leading a holy life, leading a contemplative life and going toward transforming union. In these four chapters is the essence of the spiritual life, the Christian life, and the life of holiness, all the way until you have transformation. All in these four chapters.

Transformation—what does that mean? Well, as you get closer to Jesus and approach His holiness and goodness, and the two of you are getting closer and closer, all of a sudden comes a moment when, instead of two, you've become one. This is transformation, when you and God are one. And you become one by accomplishing perfectly the will of God.

The very first sentence of John 14 says, "Do not let your hearts be troubled." Do not *let* your hearts be troubled. You know what the word *let* means? It means permit. Permit. Now, this was said to the apostles just before He died. Jesus is giving them His last will and testament. He had already washed their feet in chapter 13 and told them how Judas was going to betray Him. Now He begins to get to the meat of Christianity. He has healed the sick; He has cured the blind, the deaf, the crippled; He has exorcised demons; He has done the whole thing and even raised the dead. But He doesn't say a thing about those things right now. He's telling you and me the secrets of holiness.

"Do not permit your heart to be troubled." Now, you can't help *feeling* troubled. I don't know how you could read the papers these days, listen to the news, and not be troubled. But Our Lord keeps saying, "Don't *let* your hearts be troubled." But how are we going to keep from feeling troubled? He doesn't say, "Don't let your heart *feel* troubled." He said "*be* troubled." There's a difference. I can feel troubled, I can feel anxious, but it doesn't interfere with my trust.

And that's the next thing He tells us to do: "Trust in God still, and trust in me" (see John 14:1). You see, we're human beings, and we can't help feeling anxious about the present moment. But still Jesus keeps saying, "Don't let your heart be troubled." How am I going to keep from feeling the effects of disappointment, of anger, of somebody trying to do me in? I can't keep myself from *feeling*; feelings happen so quickly, and they linger because we're weak human beings. But that isn't what Our Lord is telling us. He's talking about when our anxieties and frustrations begin to *possess* us, when we become *obsessed* and there's nothing on our mind except the person who hurt me or the thing that's happening; when whatever it is becomes my life, my thoughts, my food. That's what

He means. And so what is the remedy for this kind of frustration and worry? He said, *trust*. "Trust in God. Trust in me." How are we going to trust when everything seems to be falling apart?

It's amazing to me how God chastises His people. We have awful things happening all over the world today: anger, threats of war, retaliation. Oh, and the worst kind of hatred, the hatred that comes right from your guts; it's everywhere. The fear of even traveling, the fear of what's gonna happen tomorrow, the fear of what they're gonna do, what we're gonna do, all of these kinds of things. You know, my friends, that's part of the chastisement. We have to know that. We're all gonna suffer from these things; you can't run, and you shouldn't be afraid. We must trust. We say, "Somebody has hurt me very bad, and I've got to take action." So we take action. But we have to be ready for the consequences of every action we take.

I have to trust that if I have done what I should do in the eyes of God, no matter who thinks I'm wrong, I must go on, trusting that He will take care and give us light. In your life and mine, things don't always make sense. When something in my life happens that just doesn't make any sense, I take it as coming from God. You say, "Now, that doesn't make sense." Well, He may not ordain it, but He does permit it. The present moment to me, more and more as I get older, more and more what comes out is that trust element. I cannot trust God if I don't see God in the present moment. If I don't see His chastening hand, His loving hand, His providential hand. I've got to see God in the present moment. I've got to see His action; I've got to see His will; I've got to see His providence; I've got to see His wisdom. You have only to read the Old Testament. When the people of God strayed, nations were against them, they suffered from famine, from slavery, from all kinds of things. All of it was only so that God could pull them back.

So when Our Lord says, "Don't let your hearts be troubled," what He is saying is that, in the present moment, be it ever so tragic, God has designed it or willed it or permitted it for some greater good, and that is the basis of our trust. So from the very first two sentences of His last will and testament, the Lord hits us hard. "Don't permit your heart to be troubled; if the whole world shall fall apart, trust me." That's an awfully big order. But we have an awfully big God.

Let's see what else He says: "There are many rooms in my Father's house" (14:2). There are many degrees of holiness. "If there were not, I should have told you" (14:2). And then He gives you the reason why you should be able to suffer whatever happens with trust—because, He says, "I am going now to prepare a place for you, and after I've gone and prepared you a place, I will return to take you with me" (14:2-3). Remember when we were talking about Heaven, as a state and as a place? Our Lord is saying it here. Everything that happens to you—good, bad, indifferent, joyous, sorrowful—all is pruning and making you grow brighter and brighter, as St. Paul says in the Letter to the Corinthians, until you are "turned into the image you reflect" (2 Cor. 3:18). Jesus is telling you, in this short paragraph, the essence of holiness.

Why does He permit the sorrowful things in your life, in my life? Why does He permit these tragedies and the disappointments? "So that where I am, you may be too" (14:3). There's the solution to all the suffering in the world, to all the loneliness, all the pain, everything that aggravates our poor human nature. The reason why we struggle so hard with our faults and weaknesses and imperfections, the reason why some things we want we never, never seem to get. Why? Because, He says, "I go to prepare you a place. There are many rooms in my Father's house, many mansions, many degrees of holiness. I want you to get the very highest; I want you to see the most glorious things in the kingdom; I want you to understand the most awesome mysteries. I want you to see my Father's face in the most glorious way. And I want you to be with me."

The essence of love is to *be with*. It is painful to be separated from those we love, so the essence of love is to be with. That is why Jesus tells us: "The reason I don't want you to be troubled, no matter what happens, is that I want you to trust that whatever happens in your life, I am with you. The reason is: I've got a place for you that you'd never dream of, that is so fantastic that no one could describe it, and when you die, I myself will come for you."

You know, I've gone to a couple of banquets, the very special kind, real highfalutin things—one in particular, where I was led in by this celebrity. I happened to be the speaker, and I was going to get some kind of award. So the thing was so special that everyone before me, when I came in with this special person and we walked down the aisle, everybody clapped. And I wondered at the time if this is what the Lord meant when He said, "When your time comes, I'm going ahead of you, so that when it's time for you, I shall return to take you with me."

Faith and trust are very akin, but trust is closer to hope, because in hoping you know that God is going to bring good out of everything that happens to you. There is, in trust and faith, that element of negative darkness: you don't know. Your understanding is many times darkened by your feelings; it's kind of in a shadow. And your will is many times weakened by the fact that you're so devastated by what just happened that you don't know what to do. So there is that element of perfect trust. Faith says, "I don't know why this happened." And there's no making up reasons. We may understand one day, but trust is at it's very highest and very best when I don't understand, and I say, "Lord, I trust You. I don't understand, but I know You love me. I know You love me and whatever is happening to me at this moment, You can bring out of it what is for my very, very best. I praise Your holy name." This is holiness. Your feelings are still there; your doubts are still there; the fact that you're in darkness may be still there; but your will has said, "I trust You, Lord."

Now, let's go on. And don't get discouraged if you don't understand all that Jesus has just said, because Thomas didn't get anything; these apostles didn't understand a thing. After the sublime four verses we just heard, Thomas comes up and he says, "Lord, we do not know where you are going, so how can we know the way?" (14:5). You know, that sentence, from someone who spent three years with Jesus in His humanity, it's almost unbelievable. So don't be discouraged if you say, "Oh, this holiness stuff is too much." Thomas didn't understand, and he was an apostle. Well, Jesus is very patient. Extremely patient.

He says again, "I am the Way, the Truth, and the Life" (14:6). You have to understand this one sentence in context with the following three sentences. He says, "No one can come to the Father except through me. If you know me, you know my Father too. And from this moment, you know him and have seen him" (14:6-7). Theologians have racked their brains for centuries, trying to figure out the Trinity: one God but three Divine Persons. In Jesus, you see the Father. In Jesus, you see the power of the Spirit. The Father brings forth His Word, the Eternal Word—Jesus—and the Word came down and dwelt among us; He was made flesh, and the Spirit dwelt within Him.

In order for me to continue to trust, I have to have my thoughts geared in other directions. I just can't be in a vacuum. If I'm having all kinds of problems and anxieties and frustrations and disappointments, I can't just sit there and say, "Well, I'm gonna give it to You, Lord, and I trust You." I've got to gear my mind in another direction more powerful than the pain I have, and He's telling us how to do that. "Come to me, all you who labor and are overburdened, and I will give you ..." What? *Rest.* (Matt. 11:28). How could He do that? Because He is the Way, the way to the Father. Because when you see Jesus, you see the Father. He Himself is the way. He shows us the way. He tells us the truth because He is Truth: everything He said, He heard from the Father; everything He did, He saw the Father do. And He is Life. "He who eats my flesh and drinks my blood" has *what* within him? *Life.* (John 6:54).

So in all of this, we learned that the only way I can trust in the midst of tragedy is to be aware of the Trinity within me. He Who is within me—the Lord God, Son, and Spirit—is so much greater than whatever is happening to me. The Trinity within you is so much more important than whatever is happening to you. So, as you continue to feel the weaknesses, the tragedies, the heartaches of the present moment, you are aware of the Way, the Truth, and the Life that transcends whatever is happening to you.

Now, here we have come again to a sublime discourse that penetrates the very clouds, Heaven itself. And now we have another dumb question, from Philip this time. Jesus just got through saying, "If you know me, you know my Father" (14:7), and Philip says, "Lord, let us see the Father and then we shall be satisfied" (14:8). In other words, "Lord, if you gotta go, go. Let me see the Father, and I'll be okay." They miss the entire point. And by this time, even Jesus, the Son of God, is impatient. And He says, "Have I been with you all this time, Philip, and you still do not know me?" (14:9).

I think you and I are very much like Thomas and like Philip. "Give me what I want, Lord. You can keep all the sublime stuff, all this interior life and Heaven. Just give me what I want right now." Have you ever said that? Sure you have. I have. We don't take time to let these sublime mysteries penetrate our hearts and our minds. We don't take time because we've got so much junk to worry about.

So Jesus has to come back again and repeat exactly what He just said. Exactly. He says, "To have seen me is to have seen the Father. So how can you say, 'Let us see the Father'?" (14:9). Here, Jesus has given us the secrets of Heaven itself, and these men were so mundane. And Jesus says, "How can you say that?" He's getting frustrated with these men. "The words I say to you, I do not speak as from myself; it is the Father living in me who is doing this work" (14:10).

Scripture is so full of the most sublime thoughts and words. You wonder how the Trinity is constituted? Three Persons, one God — it really breaks your head. But it's right here. He says, "The Father lives in me, and he's the one who does the work." We don't understand that. You see, we don't understand that the Father is in Jesus and Jesus is in the Father. We get so caught up in all the things that bother us. I know what some of you are thinking: "I'm like Philip and Thomas. I don't have it up here; I'm too dull to realize that this is an important thing or that this is sublime." Everybody is dull compared with God. I don't care if your IQ is 350; you're still dull when it comes to God. But if you place yourself before the Lord in a humble way and say, "Lord, open the mysteries to me, that I may understand," the Spirit will flood your soul with exactly what you need. Not what somebody else needed, not St. Gertrude or somebody else who could write volumes of sublime words, but just what *you* need.

And that's exactly what the Lord is saying. He says, "The words I say to you I do not speak as from myself; it is the Father living in me." You know, that's hard for people to understand. Sometimes somebody will come here to the Network, and they'll say, "Mother, you've done a terrific job." And I say to them, "I didn't do it. The

Lord did it." And they say, "Oh, come on, He used you." They don't understand. They just don't. And they didn't understand Jesus when He said the same thing. He gave all the credit—for His words, for the way, the truth, the life, the miracles, all of it—He said, "It's all the Father."

He said, "I am in the Father and the Father is in me" (14:11). And He knows He's not getting to them. He has to come up with something, so He says, "Well, if you don't believe what I'm saying, believe it on the evidence of the work I do" (see 14:11). This is the Lord saying that. Now, what does that say to you and me about the spiritual life? It says, we must have that sublime truthful humility. Not the kind of humility that has a hook to it. You know what humility with a hook is? It's when you go around fishing for a compliment, and then when you get the compliment, you say, "Oh no, that's not true." That's humility with a hook. You fish for it, you get it, and then you deny it. That's not true humility. No, it's perfect pride. In this chapter is the whole essence of the spiritual life: trust, faith, the Trinity within me, and to know that without Jesus, we are not capable of one good thing, in thought, word, or deed. We are not capable. In our press room we have a sign: "It is you, O God, who have accomplished all we have done" (see Isa. 26:12, NABRE). That's the truth, and to deny it is a lie. So now we're at John 14:12, and there's more to come, because there is no limit to what God can do, will do, and wants to do for each one of us.

And so now Jesus says something kind of serious. He's tried so hard with these people, and He says, "I tell you most solemnly, whoever believes in me …" (14:12). Whoever *believes*. Whoever believes that the Father is in Jesus and Jesus is in the Father; whoever trusts; whoever understands, even to the least degree, the necessity of knowing and attributing everything they do to the power of God within them. He says, "I tell you solemnly, whoever believes in me will perform the same works as I do myself, and he will perform even greater works" (14:12).

You see, when Jesus said, "If you ask for anything in my name, you will get it," He didn't mean to be some kind of name-dropper. There's nothing worse—to me anyway—than when somebody comes up and starts reciting all the people they know. I don't care who you know. I just want to know you. So don't be a name-dropper to the Father. He doesn't want to know that you know the name of His Son. He wants you and me to live in Jesus and Jesus to live in us, as the Father lives in Jesus, and Jesus lives in the Father. Then you will do the greater works.

What are the greater works? I mean, when you look at our human nature, what can you do with it that's greater than what Jesus did? He healed the blind. He healed the deaf. The cripples got up and walked. The possessed were delivered. Obviously, those are not the greater works, because Jesus did all these. He raised the dead. What is the greatest work? If I give my body to be burned and have not love, it's nothing. If I give away all of my possessions to the poor and have not love, it's nothing. If I can speak with the tongue of angels, it's nothing without love (1 Cor. 13:1-3). The greatest work in the whole world is when you and I cooperate with God and respond to the present moment with love and acceptance. That's much greater than healing the sick and raising the dead. What I do in the present moment—whether it's frying an egg, sweeping a floor, talking to five thousand people, or praying alone in my room—if I can do that with great love of God and neighbor (the two go together; you can't separate them), then I will have done the greater work.

Let's look at verse 13, and you will see exactly what I'm saying. He says, "Whatever you ask for in my name, I will do, so that the

Father may be glorified in the Son" (14:13). Now, we're going right back to where we were. We must give credit for every single thing we do to Jesus and to the Father. They work in us. We can't accomplish anything without that. Now, when I can do that, then the Lord is free to work. Why is He free to work? Because then pride is not going to be the fruit of the work. The worst thing that can happen to some people is to be successful. They can't take it. Some people can't take authority; they're wonderful, except if you give them authority. Then they literally fall apart and lord it over everybody; they cease to give credit to God.

Now, let's go along further. "If you ask for anything in my name, I will do it" (14:14). Now, that's the hitch. It doesn't mean that I'm gonna say, "Lord, in the name of Jesus, I want this." If you think that's what it is, you have missed the point. If I speak in your name, I've got to have your spirit; I've got to know your thoughts. I have to be totally submitted to your will, or I don't speak in your name. An ambassador from America that would go to another country and speak in his own name would be sent back so fast. He has to think the way his country thinks; he has to be what his country is. He has to symbolize it; he has to speak it; he has to think it; he has to be absorbed by it. Only then can you speak in the name of a nation. If you speak outside of the will of the nation, you are no longer an ambassador. So Jesus doesn't mean "use my name." He didn't say, "Anyone who uses my name will get what he wants." No, he says, "If you ask for anything *in* my name." Believe me, my friends, that's an awesome task. To dare ask for anything in the name of Jesus, you and I must at least make the effort. We don't always succeed, but that's okay as long as Jesus knows we're making the effort to accomplish His holy will, that we give Him the credit and the glory and the praise for everything we do, knowing He does it in us, trusting Him in the midst of tragedies and heartaches and frustrations, and when we feel all is lost. When we can look up in pain and sorrow and say, "I trust You, O God," then we may dare to speak and to ask in His name because, as the Father is in Jesus and Jesus is in the Father, They will be in me and in you.

So let's go on. In order to accomplish all of this, I must have love. The Lord has given us trust, faith. And He has told us how to hope. It is because I believe and know that the Trinity lives in me that I hope. And now He gives us the third element of holiness: love. And He says, "If you love me, you will keep my commandments. I shall ask the Father and he will give you another Advocate to be with you forever" (14:15-16). So you see, that's the answer to speaking in His name. "If you love me, you will keep my commands. If you love me, you will do my will. If you love me, you will see me in the present moment. Trust me, I know what I'm doing. Trust me."

You know, you can read all the spiritual books in the whole wide world, and they'll never tell you as much as this one chapter, chapter 14 of John. Let's go on. He talks about the Spirit of truth, "which the world cannot receive because it neither sees him nor knows him" (14:17). The world doesn't see God in the present moment. Take the present moment of today in our nation, in the world. All we see is reprisal, hatred and more hatred, terrorists and more threats of more war. It's all we see. How many of us see that God has all this in His hands and is saying, "Come back to me; stop your evil ways or you shall destroy yourself"? That's what I see. I can see that very clearly. We shall destroy ourselves, and God then will start anew, because we do not acknowledge His sovereignty.

Now, the world doesn't see this, but Jesus says, "You know him." Why? "Because he is with you, he is in you" (14:17). He is with you, and He is in you. You know, sometimes we think this is so sublime that it's a theory; it's not realistic. Or people say,

"Sure, sure, sure, Mother, I trust, but those around me don't trust."
You're not responsible for anyone else's trust. The fact that other
people around you don't trust is what forces your trust up to a
higher level. And God permits that too. Don't worry. Don't worry
about other people trusting. Don't worry about the consequences
of their lack of trusting in your life. That is also a part of elevating
your trust level.

Now, when the Lord said He's going to send the Spirit to be
in us and with us, He said the most beautiful thing; He said, "I
will not leave you orphans" (14:18). You know, a lot of people
feel like orphans although they have parents and relatives and
friends. We don't have any orphanages anymore. I don't know
why, but we don't. But the whole world is full of orphans because
we don't know God. We don't know God, and if you don't know
God, you're an orphan—because there is a kind of feeling of not
belonging. That's why I want you all to know God. You're in His
family. You belong to that Trinity. He breathed a soul into your
body. He died for you. He sent the Spirit, as it says here, to be
with you to the end of time.

"On that day," He said, when the Spirit comes, "you will understand that I am in my Father and you are in me and I am in you"
(14:20). And then I want you to hear this: "Anybody who receives
my commandments and keeps them will be one who loves me,
and anybody who loves me will be loved by my Father, and I shall
love him, and show myself to him" (14:21). These are the words of
Jesus. He didn't speak about the miracles He performed and about
His charisms that we're so caught up in today. He spoke about
the greatest work of all: to live that intimate life with God in your
heart, to trust Him no matter what, to keep His commandments.

Today, we don't have commandments. But let me tell you,
there *are* commandments, and you've *got to* keep them. On that

depends the indwelling of the Father, the Son, and the Spirit. You can't live a life of sin and holiness at the same time. We can fall and rise; that's a part of holiness. But just to lie there and act as though sin is just a way of life ... You see what happens? You miss all of this. You can go your whole life in the gutter because you want to do your own thing. Is it worth it? I don't think so. Because you're not happy. There is no permanent joy except in doing the will of God. I hope you understand a little bit the great dignity He has given us.

Remaining in God to Bear Fruit

So, we're going to continue what we were looking at last time. The four chapters in John 14–17 give us the basis of the entire spiritual life. I think we left off around John 14:21: "Anybody who receives my commandments and keeps them will be one who loves me; and anybody who loves me will be loved by my Father, and I shall love him and show myself to him." You'll notice, throughout this Gospel, throughout these four chapters, the Lord is always indicating an act of will. An act of will. He talks about *remaining*; He talks about *accomplishing*; He talks about *receiving*. All of these terms, all these phrases, are indicative that you and I have choices to make. And so He said, "Anyone who receives . . ." Now, if I have the power to receive, I also have the power to reject. "Whoever receives my commandments and keeps them . . ." The word *keep* is also indicative of some very definite effort on your part, on my part. It is also indicative that I can do the opposite. I can say, "I reject the commandments and I'm not going to keep them." The Lord is always prodding us very gently and uses such nice, soft words—so soft, sometimes, that we miss the implication.

Now, He said: "That person will love me." You'll notice, He doesn't say "everyone." The Lord is not talking to the whole mass of humanity. He said "anyone, anybody." Meaning you. He's always talking to individuals. "He will be the one ..." He didn't say: "That would be the group." No, He says, "You will be the one who loves me. And anyone who loves me will be loved by my Father." And if you're loved by the Father, He gives you a most fantastic promise, and the promise is that "I will love him and show myself to him."

Now, we come up against something rather distressing. In the midst of this chapter, we come to a very distressing incident. And isn't that true in life? You know, you can be going on so smoothly and you're loving God, and you're really handling the things that are coming day after day after day, and then the Lord slaps something on you. It's so hard. And so painful. Well, that's what happened to Jesus. All of a sudden Judas, not Judas Iscariot, asks: "Lord, what is this all about? Do you intend to show yourself to us and not to the world?" (14:22).

Our Lord is giving us the most sublime doctrine, and Judas (not the Iscariot) comes along with this blow — no comprehension whatever. This is the last time Jesus is able to speak to them as He's allowed to speak now from the Father, and it's so disappointing. It's like having everybody around a bedside where someone is dying, and the father of that family has given this terrific exhortation and the kid says, "When do we eat?" We just don't comprehend. Because I guess our minds and our hearts are filled with so many distressing things, or maybe not filled with much of anything. But there it is, another disappointment for the Lord.

The Lord this time just seems to ignore it. There comes a time in your life when you've just got to go ahead, whether they understand or they don't understand. You've got to take all your disappointments and your heartaches, and you've got to push them aside and just go. Our Lord goes on just where He was before. The Lord was going to leave, and He had picked Peter and He knew what Peter was going to do: deny Him. And He looked to His other apostles for support, and they asked one dumb question after another. You know, you just have to admire the stamina of Jesus. He is going to proclaim the word; He's going to do the Father's will, whether or not it looks like it's going any further, and whether or not these men understand.

He says, "If anyone loves me, he will keep my word. And my Father will love him, and we shall come to him" (14:23). The Lord is beautifully repetitious. First He says, "I will show myself to you," and now He's saying, "If anyone loves me, he will keep my word and the Father and I will come to him."

How does the Father come to us? I mean, does He just pop up in front of us and say hi? No. How does the Father come to us? How does He show Himself to me? There are many, many ways that Jesus and the Father show Themselves to us. The first way is in the Eucharist. Jesus comes to us in His Body and Blood, Soul and Divinity. He shows Himself to me in the Church, in the beauty of the doctrines, the dogmas, and the counsels. He shows Himself to me in the present moment. That's a little bit harder because, just like the present moment that Jesus just had, with a real disappointment, He shows Himself to me in the present moment, and He gives Himself to me in the fact that He calls me in this moment to be holy, to shake off all those imperfections.

My neighbor manifests to me *my* imperfection, not so much *his* imperfections. You see, someone comes up to me and brings out in me something that I don't want to see: impatience, anger, frustration, anxiety, jealousy. So what do I do? I blame that person. And I say, "If you weren't around, I wouldn't have these problems." Now, in fact, that has been a great gift from God. God is manifesting Himself to you. We only think of God manifesting Himself to us in joy, in consolations, in visions. But the most beautiful way God manifests Himself to me is in the present moment, when

He says, "You're awfully impatient. You're an angry individual. You judge rashly." So He manifests Himself in the very fact that I am brought up short, and I have to face myself and say to myself, "With all the light you have, you still haven't made it." God has manifested that to me in the present moment.

God manifests Himself to me in this book, the Bible, very clearly. He manifests Himself in nature. He manifests Himself in my neighbor. Now you say, "Well, everybody sees that." Do they? Does everybody see God in a tree? In a sunrise and sunset? We *know* so much now. We know how trees grow; we know why the sun rises; we know the sun really doesn't rise but is always in the same place. That doesn't take away the need for faith because faith sees beyond what my eyes see. That's why Our Lord said, "We will come to him and manifest ourselves to him and make our home in him." The man or the woman of faith sees God in the most unexpected places, sees God in the most distressful incidents, sees God in the most obnoxious things.

There's a unity of Father, Son, and Spirit, and it takes faith. It takes faith to be able to see God. And I must act upon that faith. I must act upon my faith with the neighbor who's so difficult to get along with. I must act upon my faith, not my feelings, and not what I actually see with my eyes. We're all going to be surprised when we get to Heaven—most of all that we made it. But we're going to be surprised to see so many people we thought didn't or wouldn't be up there, because we never went beyond the veneer.

"Those who do not love me do not keep my words" (14:24). It's a very strong sentence, extremely strong. It's an act of the will. Again, it's a decision I've got to make. If you don't keep His word, you don't love Him.

It bothers me, it bothers me so much when I see people going around living immoral lives, drinking, and they say they love God.

That's such a big fib. You can't be hurting somebody over and over and over and say, "I love you." You know, we hurt each other even when we're nice because we're not always conscious. There are things we're not conscious of; they're not deliberate. But we *know* we shouldn't get drunk; we know we shouldn't commit adultery and do all the terrible things that are flung in front of us and we say *yes* to. Then we say we love God.

He says, "My word is not my own. It's the word of the one who sent me" (14:24). And then He says: "The Advocate, the Holy Spirit, whom the Father will send in my name, will teach you everything" (14:26). You see, faith, hope, and love come to you at Baptism. The Spirit gives you those things; they're in seed form. And I want you to see the next word: "And he will *remind* you of all that I have said to you" (14:26). The Spirit will *remind* me. He gets down into our conscience. But you can say *no* to him over and over and over until suddenly his voice is so soft that you don't hear it anymore.

So you see, what the Lord has said so far is that I must do something, I must keep the commandments to prove that I love God, and the Lord will manifest Himself to me in all these wondrous ways. And I do that not on my own but in the power of the Spirit, Who reminds me of everything and gives me the grace, the power to do it.

And then He says, "Peace, I bequeath to you, my own peace, I give you" (14:27). Just a little later, He says, "I give you my joy" (15:11), and here He's saying, "I give you my own peace." So we are to have His peace, not my peace, not human peace. I am to have the peace of Jesus and the joy of Jesus. How are we gonna do that? How? Well, as I said to you, this is the most perfect example of the total program of the spiritual life. Because remember, the Lord didn't say *happiness*. He said *joy*. He didn't say the kind of joy that is happiness. He didn't say, "I'm gonna make you all very happy." Happiness is a happening. Believe me, sometimes it doesn't happen very often. Joy is something within. And if I have joy, I have peace. Peace in the midst of turmoil, joy in the midst of distress, because I find purpose, I find God in the present moment.

Now, Jesus is not leaving us alone. In these chapters, He's always telling us what to do, why, and how. Here comes a *how*. How do I maintain and retain peace? "Do not *let* your hearts be troubled or afraid" (14:27). The wrong kind of fear. Troubled and afraid. I can relate to that. It's difficult not to be afraid—very difficult. It's difficult not to be troubled. But you see, the Lord is not talking about feelings; He's talking about the mind. The mind. He's talking about those anxieties, the three-act plays that we play in our own minds, the projection we make of the future, all these little plays that we can concoct in our minds. What's gonna happen tomorrow? What's gonna happen next year? What's gonna happen if I do that, and what's gonna happen if I do this? And 90 percent of it never comes about.

If someone I love dies, yes, I'm going to be heartsick. The Lord doesn't say, "Go on and be happy now." That's not what He's talking about. He's talking about excess baggage. The excess baggage that you and I carry around. Past resentments. You hated this person twenty years ago; you hate him now; and you're gonna hate him twenty years from now. That's excess baggage. In fact, it's an albatross around your neck. It's cement shoes; that's what it is. You see, He said, "You heard me say, I am going away and shall return. If you loved me you would have been glad to know that I am going to the Father" (14:28). Not too many of us are happy when we know someone we love is going to die because we feel that separation; we feel grief; we feel all kinds of things. And that's okay. Don't let anybody tell you that you can't feel grieved or you can't feel this, you can't feel that. You feel it. So what are you going to *do* about it? My mother's been dead pretty soon now four years, and every so often, I feel real lonesome. I don't feel guilty over that. I just give it to Jesus. Give it to the Lord. You don't have to apologize. There's the joy of knowing she's there, with God. And the pain that she's not here. But I can never take away the joy of knowing how happy she is, gloriously happy, for the first time in her life.

Now, He says, "I've told you this now before it happens" (14:29). We're always accusing the Lord of not telling us enough in Scripture. The fact is, He told us everything. We just don't hear. He says, "I shall not talk with you any longer, because the prince of this world is on his way. He has no power over me, but the world must be brought to know that I love the Father" (14:30-31). This is his last word, a kind of last will and testament. In it I've found the whole essence of the spiritual life. Now, I want you to hear what He's said, because so many of you wonder, *Why is there so much evil in the world. Why do I have to suffer this? Why do I have to suffer that? Why does God let this happen to me? Why? Why? Why?*

The Lord is telling the apostles that He's not going be with them much longer because the prince of this world is on his way. The prince of this world is the enemy. It is the world itself; it is the flesh; it is temptation. For Jesus, the enemy was not interior but exterior: their hatred, the greed of Judas, the ambition of the Pharisees and Herod and Caiaphas, and the weakness of Pilate. All these human emotions have so taken hold of these people that they're about to do the worst crime in all of history. And you and I suffer from these very same things. And yet the Lord said, "He has no power over me." The reason it's happening is because "the world must be brought to know that I love the Father and that I am doing exactly what the Father told me to do" (14:31).

This is a solution to so many of our problems, to so many of the injustices, the prejudices, the things in our life that are so unfair, uncalled for. The things that you just scratch your head and say, "Why did this happen to me? This is stupid." And the Lord says something that seems contradictory. He says, "The prince of this world is on his way." He knew what was going to happen to Him. He knew every single moment, every agony, every pain. And yet He says, "He has no power over me." Doesn't that sound like a contradiction? Here are all these people coming, coming with clubs. He's going to sweat blood in the garden. Judas just left and is out to betray Him. He knows everything. As God, He knew every single pain that was going to happen to Him, everything He was going to endure. And He says, "The enemy is coming. The enemy is the one inspiring all this terrible stuff. But he has no power over me." Well, my idea of him having no power would mean Jesus wouldn't have to suffer any of that. To me, that would mean that the Father is just going to annihilate all these people; He's not going to let them touch His Son. So what does He mean saying that the enemy has no power over Him when they're out to get Him and they're going to crucify Him, take every drop of blood out of Him?

That's not what power is. Remember, one time our Lord said, "Do not be afraid of those who kill the body and after that can do no more. Fear him who, after he has killed, has the power to cast body and soul into hell" (see Matt. 10:28-29; Luke 12:4-5). So you see, it wasn't the suffering. The enemy had no power over the *soul* of Jesus. If you look at the shroud, you see a man who suffered intensely—scourged, crowned with thorns, crucified, every bone disconnected—and the serenity on His face is unbelievable, unbelievable. This is what He's talking about. "The enemy, though he will kill me and crucify me and let people think all evil against me, and I will look like a worm and no man, he has no power over me." Why? Because Jesus saw the Father's will in everything. "I am doing exactly what the Father has told me. Come now. Let us go" (John 14:31).

You see, no matter what happens, whether people love you or hate you, the enemy has no power over you. He may inspire other people to do you in and say all manner of evil against you, all of that. To the Lord, that was not where the power was. The power is whether the enemy would succeed in making Jesus despair or curse or find fault with the Father. But Jesus said, "No, I am going to manifest to the whole world." You see, in Jesus there were many examples: obedience, humility—to be obedient to the Father's will, to do exactly what the Father told Him to do; that was His food. "My food is to do the will of the one who sent me" (John 4:34). That's where the power is. It is with regard to the accomplishment of the will of God that the enemy wants the power, but that power Jesus never gave him, neither when He was tempted in the desert or now. That's why "he has no power over me."

And that's why, my friends, those of you who are listening, who are drug addicts, alcoholics, lead bad moral lives, are disobedient to your parents, rude, selfish—when you do these things, you open your will, you give power to the enemy, and you keep going down, down, down. That's the power. You see, that's why it's so important to praise God even in the midst of our trials, our tribulations, our sufferings, because then you give no power to the enemy, none whatever. You may look like you've lost it all. That's exactly what Jesus looked like, a worm and no man. But the enemy had no power over Him. No power. If you give the enemy your free will, as long as you breathe, you can repent. As long as you breathe, you can repent. If you give the enemy your free will, you can be so adversely affected. And even if you don't give the enemy your free will, when you start giving in to all these passions and things you do, knowing they are against the will of God, against the commandments, you don't love the Father. Now, if you make a mistake or commit a sin and you're going down, but you're sorry and you really put forth a lot of effort not to do that again, you come back up. And remember, no matter how far in sin you are, and even if the enemy has gained power over you, just an act of love, "Jesus, come and help me; Jesus, I'm sorry; Jesus, I don't want to be this way anymore," and that power is gone.

Let's go on and see what secrets the Lord is going to share. In John 15:1, the Lord says, "I am the true vine, and my Father is the vinedresser." Do you know what a vinedresser is? They trim the vine. You don't entrust that job to just anybody. Some of us don't have the talent. The Father is the vinedresser, and He knows exactly what you need shaved off. Jesus is the vine; you are the branch. The Father's will must constantly flow through you. When you say *no*, you cut off the sap. You're still on the vine, but you've cut off the sap. If you keep cutting it off, the Father comes, at death, and if you still say no to God at death, He cuts you off.

"Every branch that bears no fruit he cuts away, and every branch that does bear fruit he prunes" (15:2). Now, you thought that if you are bearing fruit, the vinedresser would leave you alone! If you don't bear fruit at all, He will cut you off, but if you do bear fruit, He prunes you. Why? Because He wants you to grow. I want you to think of yourself as part of this beautiful vine, with the grace of Jesus, the very nature of Jesus flowing through you. And you see, when you give your will over to the enemy, you cut the flow, and when the flow of food is cut off, the vine begins to shrivel. Now, repentance opens the flow. The Father only cuts it off at death, if we've made that last rejection of God.

Now our Lord says again, after He talks about pruning the branch, He says, "Make your home in me, as I make mine in you"

(15:4). Another decision. You've got to do it. You've got to make choices.

He says, "A branch cannot bear fruit all by itself" (15:4). Can you imagine a branch floating through the air? No, it has to be attached to something that can give it food and life. If you take your branch off the tree, it's dead. Now we're going to find something here: another act of will. "As a branch cannot bear fruit all by itself, but must remain part of the vine ..." I want you to look at that word. *Remain.* Remain part of the vine. You have to remain a part of the vine. It is something you must do. Making choices again. "As a branch cannot bear fruit all by itself, but must remain part of the vine, neither can you unless you remain in me" (15:4). In a matter of two sentences, the word *remain* comes up twice.

"I am the vine; you are the branches. Whoever remains in me, with me in him, bears fruit in plenty" (15:5). One, two, three times. Three times He says *remain.* I've got to *do* something, you see. I've got to make a decision that God, God's ways, God's word, is going to be the main thrust in my life. I know what you think: "We live in the world." Where do you think we're all living? We all live in the world. There's nothing wrong with the world as God created it. It's that *attitude* people have—greed, selfishness, all these other things. That's what makes the world an unhappy place. So the Lord says, "Why do you want to be unhappy? I mean, why do you spend so much time and money being miserable?" That's why He says: "*Remain.* Let your life be moved by my word. Then you bear much fruit."

Now He says, "Cut off from me you can do nothing" (15:5). It is important for us to understand that when Our Lord repeats the same thing over and over and over, we ought to listen hard. And then He says, "Anyone who does not remain in me is like a branch that has been thrown away—he withers; these branches are collected and thrown on the fire, and they are burned" (15:6).

Now, we need to ask ourselves a question. What does Our Lord mean about bearing much fruit and "without me, you can do nothing"? Sometimes fruit shows, and sometimes it doesn't. If I'm patient, it will show. But there are interior things that we do that don't show. For example, you can feel resentment coming on toward someone, and you can say, "Jesus, help me. I don't want to feel that way. I forgive that person." Nobody sees that, but that's fruit. You can have a temptation as you see the naked people on billboards, and you say, "Jesus, forgive me; I didn't want to have lust in my heart." That's fruit. Now, you may not *see* the fruit, because you're struggling so hard against temptation; you're struggling so hard against lust; you're struggling so hard against anger and hatred and resentment and guilt. But *in the struggle* is fruit; the struggle against it *is* fruit. And don't forget that. If you forget that, you're going to be discouraged twenty-five thousand times a day.

Now He says, "If you remain in me, and my words remain in you, you may ask what you will and you shall get it. It is the glory of my Father that you should bear much fruit, and then you will be my disciples" (15:7-8). And *then* you will be my disciples. Sometimes you think it sounds awfully hard to be a disciple. No—sin is hard. To overcome temptation may take a bit of misery because you're fighting hard, but you have long-range joy, courage, love, fortitude. So if you've had to struggle to overcome yourself, to bear fruit, and you've had to grit your teeth, pray hard, sweat, to overcome temptation, to say no to sin, the long-range result is that you grow in merit and holiness, and you get all of these things. Now, sin is just the opposite. You can have a lot of pleasure in a sin, but you have triple misery: you have guilt, resentment, anger. All those terrible things just crowd in upon you. Bad fruit.

And the worst part of it is that along with what you have suffered, other people have suffered. See, that's one of the big problems when we come to making choices. It's sometimes very easy, very easy to sin, and it may be very pleasurable, and you think nobody sees you. It's all a lie. It's all gonna catch up with you. The person who takes a drink, he doesn't think that's too bad; but when he chugs Bloody Marys at six o'clock in the morning, and he still doesn't see that, there's something very, very wrong; it's beginning to catch up. But you see, his senses or her senses have been so blinded and so dulled that misery becomes a part of life. It becomes a part of life. And the Lord doesn't want that. The Lord doesn't want you to go through this over and over and over and over. He wants to give you something. And He says right here what it is. He says, "As the Father has loved me, so I have loved you" (15:9). That's a lot of love.

You know what? He says the same word again: "*Remain* in my love. And if you keep my commandments, you will remain in my love, just as I have kept my Father's commandments and remain in his love" (15:9-10).

You might ask why it seems like a lot of fun things are sinful and the ways of God are hard. I don't think all fun things are sinful. And I don't think sinful things are fun. I think having a deep hatred for your neighbor is not fun. If you're talking about sex and pleasure, even that, if it's selfish and not built around God and marriage, it's lust. That's a far cry from sacramental union. It's as far as the north is from the south. The fun of sin—what you say is fun—is short-lived, extremely short-lived, because the enemy doesn't intend to give joy. He takes sin and dangles it in front of you, but he hates you when you give in. You're like a fish in the water; you get hooked. No one can tell me that is fun.

God created you for Himself, and you've got a very special part in your soul and heart that belongs only to God and that goes into an upheaval when you sin grievously—what we in the Church call mortal sin—when you shut God out. That's what mortal sin means. It means you close the door on God and say, "I'm busy. Don't bother me. I wanna have my fun." But it's short-lived because that fun repeated over and over and over again can deaden your conscience. It could make you unloving to your neighbor, make you suffer, give you diseases of every kind, if it's a moral issue. If it's anger, you can be eaten up with anger until nothing but hatred spews out of you. None of that is fun. None of that is enjoyable. And I would feel extremely bad if I thought any of you loved evil so much that you found joy in evil. You know, St. Paul says in 1 Corinthians 13 that love never finds joy in another person's sins. Well, that also means you don't find that joy in your own sins, because they offend God. How can you be joyful if you know you have just offended God?

And we just learned from Jesus: "If you remain in me, as I remain in you, you will bear much fruit. If you keep my commandments and remain in my love, the Father will come and we will make our home in you." You can't beat it. You can't beat the deep reality, also the responsibility, that you and I have. We have a choice to love God, and our neighbor, or not to love God and our neighbor.

Ask the Lord to give you that determination, so that when you fall you arise again immediately, trusting in His love, His mercy, and His goodness—and to give you that determination that you shall follow Him and keep His commandments and love your neighbor in the same way He loves you.

We need to pray for all mankind and pray that materialism does not come into our hearts and take away the fruits and the gifts of the Spirit. Let's pray every night, "Lord, make me holy. And let not the enemy have power over me. Let me see Your will in the present moment, and no matter what happens, Lord, let me at least cry out in the midst of my anguish and pain, 'I praise You, O God.'" So let's together pray for each other to be holy. We all struggle. We are all weak. We all fail. We all fall. It's in the rising that we bear fruit.

Becoming Disciples and Friends of Jesus

As I mentioned before, in John's Gospel, chapters 14-17, we have the whole spiritual life. It's amazing how the Lord told us exactly how to be holy throughout these four chapters. He gives us the secret of high contemplation, the secret of holiness, the secret of how to live a Christian life in the world, the secret of how to know God, the secret of how to understand the mystery of the Trinity, and the secret of how to bear fruit, and why we don't bear fruit. There are so many answers to so many questions in these four chapters that it just boggles the mind.

So this week we're going to continue with John 15:7. Last week, we talked about being branches on the vine. The Lord is the vine. Now, all the sap and all the life comes from the roots and from the vine. So it's very easy to see that unless you are constantly being fed by this vine, nothing's gonna happen.

So now we're going to continue: "If you remain in me, and my words remain in you — all that sap, all that nourishment from the vine — you may ask what you will and you shall get it" (John 15:7). Now, I know what you're gonna say: "Oh, come on! I have asked God for a lot of things, and I didn't get it." Well, let me tell you, there is asking, and then there's *asking*.

When you ask God for something, you must remember that you should ask for what is best for you. But that isn't always what you ask for. "What about the conversion of my daughter or my son? Or for my husband to stop drinking?" Certainly, God wants that. Yes, He does. But, you see, God in this instance has to deal with other people's wills. Your husband has to want to stop drinking; your daughter or son has to want to change their lives. So you think now that your prayers are not being answered because this conversion hasn't occurred, or you haven't gotten this job or whatever. That's not true. God is not even saying *no*. He's working on it. It *takes time* to convert people; it takes time to understand that I just can't walk in right now and get a job. There may be a better one in store. And if we don't always get an answer, the answer we want, you can be sure He's working on it.

And then there are times when there's a definite *no*. And let me show you how you can know the difference. When you're praying for someone's conversion, you know that God wants that conversion. Now, it may take a longer period of time before that conversion comes along, but you know you're asking for something that is God's will. And unless that person directly says *no* to God, you can be assured that—in your lifetime or not in your lifetime—that person will be saved. Why? Because you are definitely asking for something that is the will of God.

Now, there are other things that we aren't too sure if that's His will or not, even though we want it. Maybe I want a Cadillac, but I can only afford roller skates. Well, it's not God's will that I get a Cadillac if circumstances only give me enough money for roller skates. So we have to understand, the thing we ask of God is not always for our best. But when I am asking for someone's salvation or I'm asking for more humility or more gentleness, when I'm asking for the grace not to yield to sin or temptation, the grace is there immediately. Why? Because I am asking for something in the will of God. This is where Our Lord says here, "If you remain in me ..." If I am united to Jesus, I'm only going to ask for His will. How did Jesus pray? "Father, thy will be done on earth as it is in heaven." And in the garden, "Not my will, but yours be done." And to the apostles He says, "My food is to do the will of my Father.

So when He says, "If you remain in me, if you're close to me, if you're aware of my presence in your heart and soul, if you remain in me and my words remain in you ..." His words—the Scriptures. It doesn't mean you're going to memorize them, but the Spirit will bring the Word to mind if you just read it. If you treasure the beauty of the Eucharist, the presence of Jesus; the beauty of having such a friend as Mary, His Mother; the beauty of having the kingdom of saints in Heaven and all the beautiful people that are around us all day long ... If we remain in that aura of holiness and goodness, we will only ask for the will of God, and that's why Jesus can assure us that if I'm asking for the will of God, the will of God is done and will be done in us. And that's why He can say, "You shall get it." And it's not a contradiction. There are many times in my life I have prayed for things that I'm awfully glad I didn't get. I really am. I can say, "Thank You, Jesus, that I didn't get that prayer answered." But at the time, I just thought the Lord had abandoned me.

So you must understand that when our Lord makes this really broad statement, there are conditions to it. I have to remain in Him; His words have to remain in me; and then I only ask for what Jesus asked for. Even before Pilate, and that never ceases to amaze me, when Pilate said, "Don't you know I have power to release you and power to crucify you?" (John 19:10). And the Lord broke His silence, and He said, "Oh no. You have no power over me except as the Father gives it to you" (see John 19:11). So He wanted to correct Pilate and let him know that, in everything that was happening to Jesus at that moment, it was the Father's will. He permitted it. He permitted men to exert this fury on the Son of God, on Jesus, His Son, so that you and I could be redeemed. So, with that in mind, you have to realize that we must always pray, "Lord, I ask for this, if it is Your holy will." That's the only way you can pray. Because that's the only way Jesus prayed.

"It is to the glory of my Father that you should bear much fruit, and *then* you will be my disciples" (John 15:8). You know, these little words in Scripture — *as*, *then*, *by* — they really put a whole new picture on everything. He says, "It is to the glory of my Father that you should bear much fruit." He wants you to bear fruit. What does he mean by bearing fruit? It means that I overcome my weakness. I overcome those things that are obnoxious to other people, those things that I know myself are against the laws of God, against the commandments of God, and even these little temperament things that come along — we're just so sensitive, so jealous, so everything. We have to at least work on them. We don't always overcome, but at least there is a longer time between outbursts of anger. And everybody knows it's not you. They know the real you is hot-tempered, impatient or jealous or envious or lustful. And so when you see someone change, you say, "Oh, God is so wonderful."

So I want you to bear much fruit. God has given you His Son, Jesus, to merit the Spirit's coming into your heart and bearing that fruit in you. And *then* you're His disciples. You know there's a lot of people running around who think that as long as they say "I believe in Jesus," they can do all the craziest things you ever heard of. They can be immoral; they can lie; they can cheat; they can embezzle, but they believe in Jesus and they're gonna be saved. That is not true. Believing in Jesus is to bear fruit. That's what He says: "Bear fruit, and then you will be my disciple." To go around saying you're saved and then lie and cheat and yield to hate and gossip and all the things that are un-Christian …

Our salvation is an ongoing decision. God has given us Jesus. He has redeemed us, and He has healed us. But I've got to keep using that power and using that grace. So if I don't bear fruit—it's very definite here—I am not His disciple. I may *want* to be. Now, when we say "bear fruit," we don't mean to say we've arrived at some high degree of gentleness or the highest degree of purity or high degree of anything. It means we are striving, and even though we may fall, it's out of weakness, not a definite decision on our part. So I've got to bear fruit to be a disciple of Jesus.

"I'm saved." What happened if you committed adultery? That's ok, I'm saved. You're not saved. You've got to bear fruit. Adultery is not fruit. Don't tell me you love much, no, you don't love much, you love your pleasure and you love yourself much, but not your neighbor, not your wife, and not God. To be a disciple of Jesus is to bear fruit that will give glory to the Father. If you're going around committing adultery, you are not giving glory to the Father; you're giving glory to the devil, but not to the Father. You can't be in two kingdoms at the same time. You've got to be in one or the other; there is no middle ground. So you can't have a little bit of adultery, a little bit of faithfulness.

You might say I'm being fundamentalist. This is not fundamentalism. Jesus is telling you how to be a disciple. And He's not asking for perfection. He's asking for effort. "If you remain in me and my words remain in you, you're going to bear fruit." There are no two ways about it. It's not a matter of being a fundamentalist. A lot of these thing are symbolic. We know Jesus is not a vine; we know you're not a branch. That is a symbol. You can't take that fundamentally. You can't say Jesus is a vine, I'm a branch, literally speaking. But it shows the dependence. It's the symbol of our total dependence upon the Lord.

So we get clear in our minds what it means to be saved. St. Paul says in Romans, "In hope we are saved. It's not in sight yet. If we had it, we wouldn't have to hope for it" (see 8:24). That's what he says in Romans. So salvation is something we work on day after day after day after day, by being a disciple. "And *then* you will be my disciples." Keep that in mind, if you're tempted to grievous sin.

Now, in order to give us that impetus, that zeal to overcome ourselves—and it's hard when you feel all the desires, these passions, and you want to give in—Jesus gives us a way of overcoming. He says, "Just as the Father has loved me, so I have loved you" (John 15:9). I guess we don't think of how much it means to each of us to be able to say, "God loves me. Jesus loves me as much as the Father loves Him." We can't know how much the Father loves because we're finite. We're human beings, and it's like putting the ocean in a thimble. So you and I can hardly understand what it means, how much we are loved. Or maybe we can. When we say the Father loves the Son, that's the Spirit. That love is a Person. That Person is the Spirit, the Advocate, the One that Jesus sent down at Pentecost. So Jesus loves me as much as the Father loves Him, and that is the Spirit. So that means that all the love of God—the Father and Son are one in love—God loves me that much.

We're so busy about many things, and it's okay, that's part of living. But there must be times in our lives, like tonight, maybe tonight before you go to bed, just put everything aside, all your thoughts, all your problems, all of your trials, and just say, "Lord, teach me what it means that You love me as much as the Father loves You." That is the Spirit. And Jesus loves us that much.

I've heard people, men and women, say to me, "I want to be loved by someone with a great, deep love." Nobody can match this love. In fact, if you don't know this, if you don't at least strive to understand it more and more every day, if you don't at least get a little drop from that ocean into your little thimble, I question that we're able to love anyone consistently over a long period of time and accept their faults, their failings, their idiosyncrasies, their eccentricities, and all the other things that are part and parcel of our human nature. I question that we can persevere. And maybe that's why there's so much faithlessness today. So many men and women are not faithful to their spouses, and parents not faithful to the obligations to their children, and children not faithful to the obligation to their parents, and grandparents are shoved way out, and I wonder if the reason for all of this social evil isn't that we don't understand these two sentences. Jesus loves me as much as the Father loves Him. And that is the Spirit. He loves me with His entire Spirit. I must love you in and through the Spirit. That's what's so phenomenal about all of this.

Again, as we saw last week, the Lord uses the word *remain*. Do you remember when the Lord said, "Do not let your heart be troubled"? That means I must *do something*. I have a will decision to make. And now He says, "Remain in my love" (15:9). To remain means I must accomplish something. Again, we're on the will level. I must do something. I must have mental discipline. Today we don't have any kind of discipline in some areas, in many places. Discipline is some kind of enemy to freedom. No. Discipline is a part of freedom. Without discipline, you become wild, just wild. It's like putting your car to going 120 miles an hour in a space that won't take it. That's how we operate. So it's important that we know that I've got to have mental discipline. There are thoughts that you have and you've got to put them aside, if you're going to remain in his love. It's a matter of decision as to where I remain all day and in what kingdom I remain. I might pop over to the other kingdom through weakness, but I've got to bounce back again. Where do I remain? Where is my home? Is it in God's kingdom or the enemy's, or the world, or the flesh?

When you're young, all you youngsters out there listening to me, it doesn't catch up with you for a long time. All of you that are treating your parents so poorly; when you have children, they're gonna do the same to you. It's just a matter of time. It's a matter of time until it all catches up with you. You don't feel it now, but a man who is drinking himself to death doesn't know that his liver is slowly decaying—until one day, there's nothing left. That's when he feels it. But he doesn't know it's happening. Why do we have so many social diseases today? Because you're not conscious of it happening to you.

If I am to remain in the will of God, I have to make a decision. And the decision is: I want to be like Jesus. I want to be like Jesus. I want to have the freedom of a child of God. A lot of people desire holiness because they're scared to death of Hell. That's imperfect love. If you loved your husband just because you're afraid of him, afraid that he's gonna throw a fit if you don't have a cherry pie tonight, then you're making the cherry pie not for the best motive but because you're scared to death. But I think we need to understand that sometimes imperfect love is better than no love. It's better not to sin because you're afraid of God than to sin. But it's much more holy to not offend God because you love Him.

Our Lord uses that word *remain* over and over and over. If we were writing a book, I don't think the editor of the book would allow us to do this. But Jesus wasn't writing a book. He was teaching us. And you will find Jesus extremely repetitious. I think we explained that before. It is because, like children, we only learn by repetition. If you look at the first part of John 15, you'll see that He uses the word *remain* one, two, three, four, five times. Now

He says, "If you keep my commandments ..." (15:10). Here, He's telling me how. He's telling me *what* to do and *how* to do it. "If you keep my commandments, you will remain in my love." He tells you *why*, and He tells you what happens if you don't. And you say, "What right does He have to do that?" He created you. He is your sovereign Lord, whether you like it or not. But I hope you like it.

He says, "Remain in my love, just as I have kept the Father's commandments and remain in his love" (15:10). He's telling us: If we remain in Him and He in us, if His word remains in us, we will ask whatever we want. If we bear fruit, we will be His disciples. If we remain in His love, we will keep His commandments. If we keep His commandments, we will be like Him. Today, they've taken all the Ten Commandments and knocked them out the window. But this book, the Bible, is for all centuries. It is not dependent upon the will of man; it is dependent upon the will of God. That's from the prologue of John's Gospel. The Word did not come from the will of man, but only from the will of God (see John 1:13).

So we understand that we have a matter of will. We can never say, "Oh, I can't do that." If you ask the Lord for anything in His name that is His will, you will get it. St. John says that in his epistle (1 John 3:22; 5:14–16). I cannot ask for humility without getting it. I cannot ask for gentleness, I cannot ask to do the will of God, without the Lord giving all the grace I need to accomplish that will, to fulfill those commandments, to keep those commandments. And you can talk yourself out of it, and you can find a lot of people, a lot of ministers today, who say, "We don't need to worry about this one; you don't need to worry about that one, as long as you love." But see, that's a contradiction. You cannot commit fornication and adultery and say that you love. You love on a human level, but it's selfish. You cannot say that you love. Because He says, "If you keep my commandments, you will remain in my love." You're not remaining in His love if you don't obey His commandments. It's very simple. It's not difficult. It's people around you so often that make it seem difficult because they think you're nuts. That's the problem. We succumb to peer pressure. We succumb to the world. We succumb to what they say on television or in magazines or newspapers or whatever. But you've got to get back to the Book. And I don't mean you should be some kind of pious little monk or nun. You're in the world, but the Lord said you're not of the world (John 17:14-16). And that, my friend, is the difference.

Now, let's go on. He says: "You can do it, but you've got to remain in my love, in my word, in my commandments. Then you will be my disciples." Why does He tell us this? I mean, why would He tell us all these secrets of Heaven? That's what they are. Nobody knew this before Jesus came. The Old Testament was "an eye for an eye, a tooth for a tooth." But we would never think of such a thing, that the Father would love me like He loves His Son. Well, let's find out why He tells us. "I have told you this, so that my own joy may be in you" (15:11).

So many places you go, you see the saddest bunch of Christians you ever wanted to see. I mean they're just as devastated as those who don't know God. You say, "Well, everything in the world is in such turmoil." God knows it. It's all in the palm of His hand. That's what faith tells you; that's what love tells you. It may look a little messy, but it's right here in His hand. You can take all of history, and if you're really sincere and honest, you'll see the hand of God. And don't forget, sometimes God allows many things as a kind of correction for His people.

So it is because of joy. See, the Lord expects what I have just read to you in this fifteenth chapter to create such joy: "that my own joy may be in you and your joy [may] be complete" (15:11). Meaning, nothing can be added. And it is true. If we realized how much we're loved by God, would we ever feel guilty? No. Would we ever want to sin? No. Would we ever be nasty to our neighbor? No. Would we gossip, lie, and cheat and embezzle? No. We would never do those things. We might fall sometimes, but at least we'd know it, and we would be repentant. I'm not talking about perfection. We are all sinners, and we sin every day. The Scriptures say that the just man falls seven times a day, and the Lord said to Peter that we've got to forgive our neighbor seventy times seven times, which is unlimited. So we're not talking about imperfections. We're talking about making that effort not to fall into serious sin. And what is serious sin? Serious sin is to stray from God in a very serious matter with deliberate intent.

Although our dear Lord has told us that He has given us all that, and the keeping of all that He just said would be joy that was part of His own joy, it's difficult for us to experience the extent of that joy. Only in Heaven will we experience the extent of that perfect joy. There are times we stray; there are times our motives are not the most perfect; there are times our knowledge is not the most perfect. And St. Paul says, "The things I want to do, I don't; and the things I don't want to do, I do" (see Rom. 7:19). To hear St. Paul say that, I guess he wasn't too hot himself. Nobody, I don't think, wants to divorce himself from God. But at the same time, the gift of the Holy Spirit called fear of the Lord does not mean a servile fear, where you're scared to death of God. It means that you love God so much, you don't want to hurt Him. Ask the Spirit every day, "Lord, give me the fear of the Lord. Teach me that You are Father."

You know, some people in this context ask: Where does weakness end and deliberate separation begin? Well, it begins when you know this will offend God, when you know it's against His commandments, that it's a very serious matter, and you make a decision that you're going to do it anyway. But sometimes that's not the case. Many times, offending God is not the motive. But you see, if you *know* ... That's where faith comes in. Faith comes in so that whether you understand or not, whether your motive is good or bad, faith will come and separate the good from the bad, because faith says, "I don't need to understand. I know the Father does not want me to do this. I know that if I do this particular thing, it's going to harm my family, so I am not going to do that." God will always give you the grace to strengthen your will if you ask for it at the moment. You have a conscience. Unless you've killed it, you have a conscience, and that conscience will tell you, in a soft movement of the Spirit, "Don't do this. It's just going to hurt you. This is going to hurt your wife, your husband, your children." Well, you see, when we don't listen to that Spirit and we say, "Oh well, what's the difference?" then we begin to go overboard.

So often what begins by being a weakness ends up in a deliberate choice, and that's what you need to watch. And that's why humility is so important, to rise after every fall as quickly as possible. If you're Catholic, go to Confession if you have a grievous sin on your soul, so that you can remain in His commandments, remain in His love. If something is a venial sin, every time you go to Communion, that's all forgiven. Every time you say, "Jesus, I'm sorry," it's all forgiven. It's important that we repent often during the day. It's important that we say to God, "I'm sorry; forgive me." It's important that I say that to my neighbor.

Let's go on and find out exactly how to make that joy as complete as possible. But first, I think we have to know whether in this life that kind of joy is attainable or not. Yes, yes. All of our life is a struggle, and we progress every day, day after day, minute after minute. The days you think you haven't made any progress, you may have made more than your whole life. So the important thing is that, when we have become habituated, in the habit, of attaining, of doing and accomplishing the will of God in the present moment, that's where joy is. So whether something is to our liking, and whether we feel good about it or bad about it, we are happy and we're joy-filled in the fact that God's will is being accomplished, even though it is not mine. When I can reach to that point, looking for God and seeing God, seeing His love for me in the present moment, no matter what happens, then I will have perfect joy.

I have to tell you that story of St. Francis, what he told Brother Leo. They were going to a monastery, and it was cold and snowing, and he said, "Brother Leo, do you know in what lies perfect joy?" And Brother Leo said, "No, father." And Francis said, "If we go to the monastery and the monk opens the door and he says, 'Get out of here,' and he slams the door in our face, and we can say at that point, 'I praise You, Lord.' And then if we all knock again, and the brother comes out and he throws us into the snow and leaves us there all night, cold and hungry, and we can say, 'Praise You, O Lord.' In that lies perfect joy."

We can feel sad, we can be hurt, and still have perfect joy, because joy is not a happening; it is something deep inside, a contentment. Joy is a contentment, a satisfaction that God's will is done. I may not like it; it may cause me pain and suffering, but I can say with joy, "My will, Lord, is not done. I thank You. Your will is done." We don't have to think this is saved for some with mystical graces. This is for everybody. The more I fight against the will of God in my life, the more miserable I'm gonna be. It's that simple.

And in order to safeguard our joy in the midst of pain and sorrow, the Lord gives us another secret. He says, "This is my commandment: love one another, as I have loved you" (15:12). That word *as* puzzled me for years. I used to meditate on how I'm going to love my neighbor as much as Jesus loves me, as much as the

Father loves us. How am I gonna do that? The only way to do that is to love with the same love that the Father loves: the Spirit. Let the Spirit in you love your neighbor. Let the Spirit in you respond to the Father's love for Jesus. Let the Spirit in you respond to the Son's love for the Father. The Spirit *is* that love. So when Jesus said, "I send you another Advocate" (see John 14:16; 15:26; 16:7), He sent us the Spirit. I must love you with the love of the Spirit.

And then He says, "A man can have no greater love than to lay down his life for his friends. You are my friends, if you do what I command you" (15:13-14). You see, this repetition again: "If you keep my commandments, my Father and I will come and dwell in you. If you love me, if you keep my commandments, you will be my disciple; remain in my love. If you keep my commandments, you are my friend." None of us would like someone to say, "I love you" and then do something nasty to us. What makes you think God is any different? You don't like somebody doing nasty things to you and then coming back and saying, "I love you." It's hypocrisy. What makes us think we can do nasty things to Jesus in our neighbor and commit grievous sin and then say to God, "I love you"? It doesn't make sense.

We are His disciples, if we do His will. We are His friends, if we do His will. And He says, "I shall not call you servants anymore" (15:15). In the Old Testament, we were servants. But with Jesus, I am a friend of God. Because a servant doesn't know the master's business. All of these verses that we've read so far are the secrets of God. It's the Master's business. He's let us in on the Master's business. He's let you and me peek into the secrets of the kingdom. He's let you and me peek into the heart of the Father. He has opened up the kingdom of God in Heaven so that we may repeat it on earth. We are a long way from having any kind of Heaven on earth, but it isn't because God doesn't want it. It's because we're greedy, ambitious, hateful, lustful. And that's all of us. No matter what happens in the world, we all are part of the world. And so when we cry out to God, we don't say "have mercy on them" but "have mercy on us." We're all part of the human race. We're all part of the Mystical Body. And so you and I must rise above, so that we are friends of Jesus.

"You are my friends, if you do what I command you.... I call you friends, because I have made known to you everything I learned from the Father" (15:14-15). Isn't it wonderful how the Lord has given us the whole secret of the kingdom? These chapters are just fantastic. In the other books of Scripture and the other chapters of all the Gospels, you see the *works* of Jesus: performing miracles, healing the sick, raising the dead, and doing all of those things that we've mentioned before. And there are things that seem to be beyond us, although He promised us we would do even greater things than these. It's a greater thing not to commit a sin, to choose God above the enemy, over the enemy. To choose God over your own self. Our Lord says right here, "A man has no greater love than to lay down his life for his friends." You and I are not called upon often to lay down our life for our friends. But we may have to lay down our pride; we may have to lay down our selfishness; we may have to lay down our greed and lust. There is no greater love, when you give up those things for the greater good of mankind and the good of the kingdom.

Love One Another as I Have Loved You

We're on our fourth talk in a series on John 14–17. In this last testament of Jesus is the entire spiritual life. It gives us so much that you don't get particularly in the other Gospels during the ordinary life of Jesus. During His life, mostly we learned how to act on the outside of us with people, with events, and seeing the Father's will. In this last testament of Jesus, He tells us how to become holy as He is holy. How to react *inside*. This is where it's important. Everything outside is important—if I give you a cup of cold water—because *inside*, I give it to Jesus, and you receive it from Jesus. So it concerns the whole person. He has already told us to be kind and loving and compassionate and not to judge, but here He says, "Love your neighbor in the same way I love you."

Last week, we ended on John 15:15, where Jesus says, "I call you friends." You don't call everyone a friend. Some are acquaintances. Every man, woman, and child in the world is literally your brother and sister, so you have that family affinity. But the Lord says here, "I don't call you servants anymore. I call you friends." Friendship is a different relationship. You can be a brother or sister and not be a friend. In fact, some of you married people, you're married to each other, but you're not a friend to each other. That's a big difference. Because when you're a friend, you listen; you care with a special care and you're attentive, generous, listening. So the Lord wants us to know that He is our friend and we are His friends.

And in order to impress this upon us, knowing our pride, He wanted us to know *why* we are a friend. We might get the impression that we chose Him. He says, "You did not choose me; no, I chose you" (15:16). You know, it is wonderful to be chosen. All you kids that are listening, you want to be chosen for the basketball team, and you want to be chosen for the football team, and then you want to be chosen to be a halfback, and you want to be chosen to go to Harvard or Yale, or some college. And so it's very important to you that among a great group of people in the world, you are chosen. Well, the Lord knows that's important to us. Because when you say, "I choose you," it means you're special. And so He says, "You did not choose me; I chose you." Why? Why did Jesus choose you and me? I have what I feel is a fantastic vocation. And I've asked the Lord so many times, "Why, Lord, did You give us this wonderful vocation, where I can go before the Blessed Sacrament whenever I want and sit in Your holy presence?" I have to realize over and over and over, He chose me, probably because He couldn't find anybody worse. He couldn't find anybody worse, and God looks upon those who are in need.

Now, we find out *why*. He says here, "I commissioned you" (15:16). For what? Why would God choose you? First of all, He chose you to *be*, out of maybe sixty million people who might have been. You know, everybody's running around the country and running around the world looking for their identity. *Here* is your identity. This is who you are. You don't need to run around trying to figure out *Who am I?* It's all here, in St. John's Gospel, who you are. You're a child of God, chosen, special. Before time began. Imagine. Before there was a blade of grass, when there wasn't a star, there wasn't a raindrop, God knew you. "I love you and chose you and commissioned you."

So many people today feel useless. There's no such thing as anyone being useless. The only thing useless is when we choose sin over God, which makes our soul vegetate. God gave you a mind. He gave you memory to remember, an intellect to discern, and a will to accomplish, and so He wants you to understand why you were born—and to know how terrible it is when you make a decision that someone will not be born. And so it is important that you know that the reason He commissioned you is "to go out and bear fruit, fruit that will last" (15:16). So that doesn't mean you make the effort just today. It means you've got to make that effort every day. Every day, every day. "That's hard," you say. "I get tired." My friends, virtue means I choose God over myself. It may be difficult for a short time, but it has long-range fruit, long-range benefits. But sin, and pleasure that is sinful, has very short pleasure and very long pain, very long. Sometimes, for one mistake, you suffer your entire life. One mistake. But we need to understand that with God's grace, even that one mistake can be made into a stepping stone, a springboard for holiness. For goodness. And that's why He commissions us to go and bear fruit.

When we say "bear fruit," what do we mean? There are various kinds of fruit we can bear. There's witness fruit. Say, for example, a man is an alcoholic and begins to understand that he's not only hurting himself but his family, his neighbors, the people he works with, but most of all, God. You know, that's another kind of funny thing today. People say, "I'm not offending anybody if I commit adultery. I'm not hurting anybody." Come on. You've got to be kidding. There's no way you can commit adultery and say you're not hurting anybody. You hurt your wife, your children, society by your bad example, and you hurt yourself. And most of all, my friends, you hurt God. Whenever you destroy what God made, and you defy the Lord God with your "No, I shall not obey," you take away from Him the glory that the Lord spoke of: "It is to the glory of my Father that you bear fruit." It's not for yourself. It's for the glory of the Father that you bear fruit.

This is the whole purpose of being a Christian: to bear fruit. We Christians, do we bear fruit? Do you think there would be so much animosity between denominations, Baptists, Methodists, Presbyterians, Catholics, Jehovah's Witnesses, if we were really bearing fruit? We are a disgrace to the world. Why? Because we have a Gospel that says "Love one another," and we haven't even begun to love one another. You hear this minister speak against this denomination, you hear that minister speak against that denomination, and we call that love. That's not love. That's paganism. It's idolatry. To tear down what God has built up in His Son, Jesus, is not love.

Our Lord wants fruit that will last. I think all of us have to ask ourselves: "Am I bearing the fruit that will last? Am I really striving to be loving and kind and patient and understanding? And most of all, am I trying to love much?" To love much. Because without love ... St. Paul says very explicitly: "I can have a tongue of angels, and without love, it's nothing. If I gave my body to be burned and had no love, it would be nothing" (see 1 Cor. 13:1-3).

So, first of all, you and I were *chosen*. Secondly, we have been *commissioned*. For what? To *bear fruit*: "Fruit that will last; and then the Father will give you anything you ask him in my name" (15:16). And what is the fruit? "What I command you is *to love one another*" (15:17).

That's the most important commandment in the whole world. Why? Well, because God is love. And when we are asked to love one another, when I am asked to love others in the same way that God loves me, then I am asked to be like God. I am asked to be

God to my neighbor. I am asked and given the opportunity by God to be transformed into His image. In order to accomplish this one commandment, Jesus came, lived, and died, so that He could merit for you the Holy Spirit, Who is love.

Let's look at this again. First, we look at God the Father. And the knowledge that God has of Himself is the Son. And the love that exists between the two is the Spirit. So we have one God, but Father, Son, and Spirit. The image of the Father is the Word, and the love that exists between the Father and the Son is the Spirit. Now, the Spirit is a power. Love is a power. Love creates; love transforms. Love changes people, changes societies, changes families. Where there is no love, there is no change. There is nothing creative without love. Everything shrivels and dies without love, because everything was created by love. And God has asked you, a little creature, to be like Him. This commission here, these two sentences in St. John's Gospel, are the essence of life. It is what created you. Love is what created the world because love shares. Love gives. Love listens. So without love, there is no life. That's why when the husband and wife join together in sacramental union, it must be in love, and the fruit of love is a child. But you see, when you destroy all of that by selfishness and pleasure, saying, "We won't have the child, we're going to destroy the child," you see how selfish that is, because then you destroy. You say, "I want the pleasure, but I don't want the love." You can't separate them.

So love is a power. Love created you. Love made you a friend. Love commissioned you, and love commands you to love. There is no other way. Because if I don't love and you don't love, then it's every man for himself. You see, we get more and more and more selfish. And it's true, sometimes love causes pain. I think all love causes pain. Jesus came into the world and suffered greatly, from the time He was born in a stinking, smelling cave. We've got sheep and goats, and they stink. And Jesus was in a cave that had an ox, sheep, and donkeys probably, and they were probably there for days or months. They didn't go around cleaning it up real nice, so it stunk where He was born. So love has been painful from the beginning. Perhaps you think your love isn't painful. Just think of somebody you love right now. What are you going to do when they're gone? When they die? If they go downtown or they go on a trip, you're worried sick because they may get in an accident. Love causes pain.

And the beauty of love is that it is sacrificial. Without sacrifice … That's why a lot of marriages don't work today. When sacrifice ends, love grows cold—very cold. If you're not willing to give and give and give, if you're going to calculate everything—I give one, you give one; I give two, you give two—well what happens when you give four and they give one? You say, "No love." It's simple.

Maybe love isn't simple, but it is a command. He didn't say, "I would like you to love. I think it'd be nice if you loved." No, He commanded us to love. So we understand that the Lord wants us to be as much like Him in this world as it is possible. And the Lord, later on in this Gospel, calls it a new commandment. Why is it new? Well, because the old commandment to love was that I was to love you as much as I love me. Well, that's not too much. So if I'm supposed to love you as much as I love me, what happens if I hate me? You know why a lot of people find it hard to love today? Because they don't love themselves. If you don't love yourself and you don't know that you carry within you a temple of the Holy Trinity, if you don't love yourself and know your dignity and know you've been chosen by God, if you hate yourself for whatever reason, you're going to be a Marxist to everybody. Because you can't give what you don't possess.

So it's necessary, then, that you don't go even steven; you must be willing to give all you have. Even if everyone else gives nothing. Your time, your energy, your love. You see, when you love, something happens to your soul. It isn't something you do, but something that happens to your soul. So if I give you a cup of cold water ... And that's what's nice about the Lord. He didn't say just to give a cup of water; he said cold water. "Whoever gives you a cup of cold water in my name gives it to me" (see Matt. 10:42). It's very simple. So the Lord is saying that something happens in my soul. You don't see what happens to your soul. But you can see sometimes. We had a beautiful sister; Jesus radiated out of her, because she gave herself and she loved Jesus. You can't be in love and it doesn't show. That's the witness that glorifies the Father, that we read about in verse 8.

And now we're going to go on. The Lord knows that when you become a loving, forgiving, patient, caring person, the world is going to hate you. What do we mean by "the world"? The physical world is beautiful. That is not what the Lord meant by "the world." By "the world," He means attitudes of worldliness—that attitude that means we think of only ourselves, that selfishness, when we're greedy, when we look only for pleasure, when we're rude and we don't care and we'll walk over anybody to make a step up. And so in business, people will lie. You know that amazes me today; it amazes me how people lie. They look you right in the face and lie, and you know they're lying, and they know they're lying. People say what they think you want to hear. They don't care what's true. If they think you want to hear this, they'll say it, whether they believe it or not. That's the world. The world looks out for pleasure. The world looks out for self. The world doesn't care about eternity or sacrificial love or patience or kindness.

I went through a revolving door not too long ago and almost got trapped because a young man went ahead of me and pushed so hard that I practically fell out. He saw me coming. He had to see my braces. I suppose he was in a hurry. But there's no excuse for rudeness. "Out of the way. I gotta go where I gotta go. I don't care if you get there."

Now, when you come along as a Christian and you have other ideas, the world hates you. But the Lord said not to get excited about that. Nothing to worry about. "If the world hates you, remember that it hated me before you" (15:18). Now, when we talk about the word *hate*, we're not necessarily saying, "I wish you were dead." The word *hate* here indicates an uneasiness, a great distress. For example, many of you live or work in offices and some big shot comes along, who may be your boss, and he tells one of these smutty, dirty, filthy jokes that is supposed to be so funny, funny, funny. If they could see how their soul blackens and shrivels with the dirty joke, they wouldn't think it was so funny. Well, if someone in the office is a good Christian and they know he doesn't like jokes, it makes them feel extremely uneasy and they may hate him, meaning they just wish he wasn't around. They're not going to bury him; they're not going to kill him; but they're going to make him a little bit miserable. Why? Because he bothers their conscience. And you remember a minute ago we talked about the witness that is fruit, and sometimes this witness will provoke ridicule: "What are you, a holy one? Come off of it. You know, this is a modern-day age. You're living in the twelfth century." Or they belittle you and say, "Oh, I had this great joke to tell, but then here's Joe, and you know how he is, the Christian." Patronizing. Or they come up to you and say, "Who do you think you are? You have more faults than I do." They try to bury you in their own filth. They don't see their own filth. That's the world. And if you don't have the guts to fight it, they'll bury you in it.

"If you belonged to the world, the world would love you as its own" (15:19). So if you liked all these dirty jokes and all the stuff that they throw at you, then you would be one of the gang. The Lord is very modern. Very modern. And so He says, "If you belonged to the world, then the world would love you as its own." That's where it's so important to understand that you've got to stand alone before God. Because when you die, your buddies are not gonna be there. You're gonna face God all alone. If there's a million people who die the same moment you die, you're gonna be facing God all alone, and there's gonna be no excuses. You're either in His image or you're not.

That's where we fail. We succumb to pressure—to peer pressure, to worldly pressure. We get tired of them saying, "Here comes the holy one." You may be the only Jesus your neighbor will ever see. In an office of filthy jokers, you may be the only Jesus those people will ever see. You may be the only chance they'll ever get to see something beautiful, something good.

And there are ethical situations that are just as hard. Jokes aren't the worst thing. When your boss says, "You mean you don't have a mistress? That's not manly." Remember, you are not *of* the world. You are *in* the world but not *of* the world. And I think there are times when they have to know where you stand. You have to have an active response. You can lovingly say, "No, I don't. And if you have a mistress, I think your soul is in danger." I'd tell him. You might say, "Mother, you're so uncharitable." I'd rather go to Purgatory for being uncharitable than have him going to Hell because I didn't tell him the truth. Or maybe I'll go because I didn't have the guts, because human respect held me back. I have to love my brother enough to correct him. Now, after I've corrected him, as the Scripture says, two or three times, I don't have to run up and say, "Now what are you doing?" But when the opportunity comes, I have a responsibility to spread the Word of God. "I commission you to go out and bear fruit."

It's very simple, but believe me, you gotta watch the simple stuff in this Gospel, because it's pretty heavy.

"Because you don't belong to the world, because my choice withdrew you from the world" (15:19). You had nothing to do with it. You had the choice of saying *yes* or *no*, but *He drew* you. "Because you do not belong to the world, because my choice drew you out of the world, the world hates you. Remember the words I said to you: A servant is not greater than his master" (15:19-20). If you think you're greater than the Master, you belong to the world. You know, there's nothing like a good dose of a flu to make you know who you are and what you are. You're just lying there. You ache all over. You're just so sick. You're helpless. And it's good sometimes that the Lord does that to us because we get pretty cocky. He's always reminding us, "I chose you. It's my choice that makes you different."

"If they persecuted me, they will persecute you" (15:20). What does it mean? Do you remember how, when the Lord would go into the temple, they would say all kinds of things to Him? Why are you so surprised when it's hard for you to be a Christian today? Why do you want to water it down? You know, you can't put oil and water together. The oil floats. You can't mix oil and water. The world is water; God is the oil.

Now, some people say, "Well, I didn't ask God to choose me." To be chosen by God is a *privilege*. You can say *no* to the privilege, or you can say *yes*. Your free will is not interfered with. Now, you may find that kind of frightening. But how can you be frightened to be called to be love? That's all He asks. To be chosen to be love to your neighbor. To be chosen to give comfort. To be chosen to give of yourself. To be chosen to understand, to listen, to give hope where there's despair. Isn't that where your will wants to be? Isn't that what it wants to do? I would think so.

He said, "If they kept my words, they will keep yours" (15:20). Remember how He said one time to the apostles, "If they don't listen to you, go to the middle of the road and shake the dust off of your feet" (see Matt. 10:14). Shake the dust off your feet. How do you like that? So that means you do your best, and if they don't listen, you leave them to God.

Our Lord is so kind. He's always explaining things to us. And He does it over and over. He's going to explain something else now. He says that the reason they're going to persecute you is because they persecuted Him. It is on His account, not yours, so you don't need to feel guilty. If people hate you or dislike you or criticize you because you are a disciple and a friend of Jesus, you don't need to feel guilty because they're going in the wrong direction. Because it's not for your sake that they hate you. It's for His sake. I want you to get that, because a lot of you stray and become one of the crowd because you're afraid, thinking, "If I persevere in being a Christian, I'm going to make all of these people fall away from God, or they're going to hate me, or I'll be responsible for their sins." Forget it, forget it. "It will be on my account that they will do all this, because they do not know the one who sent me" (15:21). You're free. You can be a Christian and love and be free. If someone doesn't like it, you're not guilty of that. You're not guilty of anything.

And then you've got to realize that a lot of people who criticize you and hate you for being what you are don't have the light and never did. So we can't judge the light they have. Neither can we say, "I won't give them light and then they won't know, because that would be culpable ignorance." That means you're making the decision that if they have the light, they won't use it. Now, you can't do that. In Ezekiel, the Lord is very strong. He says that if you see a brother and you don't correct him, then you're going to be responsible for him. And by the same token, if you see a brother doing something wrong and you reprimand him or you lead him and give him light and he follows, then you benefit by his salvation. The Gospel is not an easy book. It is a loving book. "If I had not come, if I had not spoken to them, they would be blameless" (15:22). But now He *has* come. Praise God.

Well, I love you. God loves you. I hope you love me because it is in love that we are like God. It is in love that we resemble God. It is in love that we witness to God. It is in love that we give each other hope. I love you. God loves you. And I ask that you love your families and love your brothers and your sisters. Put love into your family, and your family will change. And if no one else changes in your family, just keep pouring in love and let the Spirit of God, the brightness of His light, dispel all of the darkness.

The Gift of the Spirit

This is part 5 of the teaching series on the secrets of holiness given in John's Gospel, chapters 14-17. So, we're going to start where we left off. Our Lord was talking to the apostles about the hostile world. It isn't often that we say the world is hostile, because we're trying to make everything look good; we're trying to make everything seem good. We say things will pass and "this is okay and that's okay," although we know they're wrong. Many things in our life, many things in our family's life or our neighbors' lives, we know they're wrong, but we kind of push them under the rug, and we say everything is wonderful. Well, it's not.

We live as Christians in a hostile world. Because as soon as you come up with your Christianity and your concepts of Christianity and what the Lord wants you to do in this day and age, and in your particular life, the world becomes hostile; it bristles. Because the world's teaching is contrary to the law of God. Now, I'm not saying it's necessarily a sinful teaching, but it doesn't teach you the things that are in this Gospel, so it's contrary. I'm not talking about the physical world, like the trees and the birds and the bees and everything that God made. That's beautiful. It's the *attitudes* of the world. It's the teaching of the world: "Eat, drink, and be merry, for tomorrow you die." But the Lord, you see, is contrary to that. He talks about pain and suffering and sacrifice and being gentle and loving and compassionate. The world says, "That seems like an awful lot of work. No, you've got to give in to yourself." So you see, it is a hostile world.

The Lord told us: "If they persecuted me, they will persecute you too" (John 15:20). They didn't like what Jesus said. They fought against it. In fact, they hated what He said to the point that they tried to, and did finally, kill Him. That's what the Crucifixion was, killing the Son of God. Now, it was used by the Father for our redemption, but it was no less a terrible thing. So Jesus' teaching when He was here was terribly aggravating to the Pharisees, Sadducees, and all the people who were of the world, because He made them think, *Wait a minute, we've got to feed the poor, not push them aside, not walk all over them.* He said, "You have to look after them. You have to love your enemy." And the world says, "No, no, no, no, no. You destroy your enemy." And Jesus said, "You must love your enemy; you must forgive them." The world says, "No, you must take revenge." So you have this constant hostility between you, your faith, and the world.

So the Lord explains, "If I had not spoken to them, they would have been blameless" (15:22). Now, a lot of you are saying, and I've heard you say it, that all the people in various countries, in third-world countries, who really have never had the opportunity to know Jesus, that they're going to be damned. I don't believe that. The Lord right here says, "If I had not spoken to them, they would be blameless." They've never had an opportunity to hear the Word. You and I have not spoken the Word, so they're going to be blameless. God will judge them by the light they have, even though that light is very different, in no way like the light in this Gospel. They have never had the Gospel preached to them. Now, a question comes up. If everyone has a sense of sin, even if they don't know where it comes from, do they truly not know where it comes from? Yes. There are a lot of people who have never heard of the Ten Commandments. We've had anthropologists and archaeologists and all the people that go into the jungles and find tribes that have been there for centuries and they've said that in their hearts is a kind of code, a moral code, maybe not like yours and mine, but there is a kind of Ten Commandments, and they follow. And there is in their heart a knowledge and understanding of a Supreme Being. They may not call Him "God," but every man, woman, and child has those two things. So they have reasons to choose the Supreme Being over themselves.

Now, the Lord says, "Anyone who hates me hates my Father" (15:23). Why? Because anyone who sees Jesus, sees the Father (14:9). So if you hate the Son, you cannot possibly love the Father. You can't because they're one God. Three Persons, but only one nature. In Jesus, there was the human nature and divine nature, but there is only one Person, only one personality, and that personality was divine. That's why it's so ridiculous when people say Jesus didn't know who He was. That is just impossible. He knew who He was from the first moment of His conception, because the divine and the human were wedded together, and never for a moment were they separated. So it's impossible for Jesus not to know who He was. People say He didn't know until He was twelve, or He didn't know until the Cross, or He didn't know at all. It just doesn't make sense. As God, there's no way He couldn't know He was God. And His human nature was not blinded. He grew in grace before God and man; His human nature grew in the knowledge of the ways and the sufferings of the world. That's what grace is. Grace is that moment-to-moment living, experiencing life in the light of God, and Jesus had that, and He grew in it. And as

He grew older, He experienced more, and that's why we can relate to Jesus so well. There's nothing I have, no suffering, no pain, no sacrifice demanded of me, that I could not go to Jesus with, and He understands. And Mary is the same; there's nothing you could suffer that she doesn't understand.

Now, Jesus goes on to explain why these people are culpable. What does *culpable* mean? It means responsible. "They have no excuse for their sin" (15:22). I can't say, "Oh, I didn't know You were the Son of God." No. Jesus says, "If I had not performed such works among them as no one else has ever done, they would be blameless, but as it is ..." (15:24). As it is, they're responsible. I want you to understand that, and I want you to think about that. You know, some of us have a colossal ability to make excuses. We are the best people in the world to make excuses. Not for others; we have a hard time making excuses for other people. We know *exactly* why they do things. We judge their motives; we judge their reasoning; we judge everything. And we're sure we're right when we're 99 percent wrong. But we give ourselves a tremendous amount of leeway when it comes to ourselves. We can excuse ourselves out of everything.

And Jesus says, "Oh no, no. If I had not performed such works among them as no one else has ever done, they would be blameless; but as it is, they have seen all this and still, they hate both me and my Father" (15:24). Now some of you are saying, "Well, I'm glad I'm saved. I've never done that." But do we really follow the Gospel? Do we really trust Jesus with our whole heart? Do we really love our neighbors as God loves us? Are we really compassionate and loving? You say, "You're asking too much." No, I'm not asking anything. This is what it says here. And I don't mean we're going to be perfect at it. No, I'm talking about that effort, and the knowledge of what I should do. Don't fall into a culpable

ignorance, which means I don't want to know and that way I won't
be responsible. You're responsible by the very fact that you have
said, "I don't want to know," which means you're going to cut off
all knowledge of God because you're afraid. You see, that's what
happened to these Pharisees. They *knew*. They knew Jesus. But
they didn't want to give up their little positions and going down
the street and having everyone say, "Oh, here is the rabbi" and
bowing profoundly. They were so attached to that. They weren't
about to give that up for humility.

You have responsibility not only toward God but toward each
other. Your relationship with God has to be long, deep. But if
you know the Father and Jesus, your relationship with them can't
remain purely vertical. Why? Because the essence of love is to share.
It is to share. And so whatever goes up and down in our relationship with God must go out horizontally. So, as you begin your
relationship with God, suddenly it goes this way, and suddenly it
goes this way, and now you've got a cross. You've got a cross, and
that's your daily cross, the daily cross that Jesus told you to carry
for Him. Now, the Pharisees, they just wanted a vertical relationship with God; they weren't bothered by anybody else. And some
others just wanted a horizontal relationship with their neighbor.
But if you just want a horizontal relationship with your neighbor,
with no strength from God to persevere in loving your neighbor,
you're going to wither. You've got to have both. The Father, the
Son, and the Spirit, one God in your soul, directing you in the gift
of the Spirit and making you go out to your neighbor.

"But all this was only to fulfil the words written in their Law:
They hated me for no reason" (15:25). Does this mean that all these
people *had to* hate Jesus, they had to do all these things, and then
Jesus makes them responsible? Is this some kind of great big theater
play, where God makes some characters wicked and He makes some

good, and then He says, "Oh, I wrote the play, and now I'm gonna tell you the acts"? Oh, that's monstrous. And yet He says: "It was to fulfill the Law, to fulfill the words of Scripture." Well, now there's something you forgot: to God, all things are present. There is no past and no future. Everything from the beginning of Creation, to Adam and Eve, to Abraham and Moses and Jacob and all the rest, to John the Baptist, to this very moment as I sit in this chair talking, all is present to Him. He saw what the Pharisees would do. He saw the hardness of their hearts, and He inspired His prophets to write it down. And it was fulfilled, not because He made it happen but because their free will chose to do this, and God saw it and brought out the most marvelous gift in the world: Redemption.

Now, He says, "When the Advocate comes, whom I shall send to you from the Father ..." (15:26). This octave of Pentecost, we ought to thank Jesus for the Spirit. We ought to say, "Lord Spirit, come into my heart. Give me Your seven gifts. Give me that one gift I need the most." And what will the Spirit do when He comes? "The Spirit of truth who issues from the Father, he will be my witness" (15:26). How will He be witness? By enlightening the minds of men that Jesus, Son of God, is Messiah, Lord of all.

Now comes a beautiful attribute of God, shining forth. He goes on and says, "You too will be my witnesses" (15:27). You know, one of the things I marvel at about God is His ability to share what He is. Not what He *has* but what He *is*. It's so hard for people to share what they are, who they are, rather than give you a buck. Maybe they'll give you a sandwich, if you're hungry. But they don't often give of themselves, give of the very stuff that's within. They want to hide that, keep it. They don't want to sacrifice and wear themselves out.

The Lord says, "You too will be witnesses, because you have been with me from the beginning" (15:27). You say, "Well, I haven't been with Jesus from the beginning." You have from *your* beginning. "Well, I didn't know Jesus till I was twenty-one." That is your beginning. You may have been born into the world, but life began when you began to know Jesus. The time you began to really know Jesus, when He became so personal to you at that moment. Or if you're Catholic and baptized at birth, the time that you had your First Communion and it was so special, and your Confirmation and that was special. And you began to go through life with all its heartaches and all its sufferings, and every time you went through something, you began to know God, to experience God, to experience His hand upon you, His love, His compassion, His care, His mercy. You began to know God. To me, these are all new births. I don't think you can say, "Are you saved?" We are saved over and over and over and over. We have a new birth over and over and over in the spiritual life. Because you just can't stay in one place in the spiritual life. You're either going forward or backward. No one stays in one spot in the spiritual life. You're either going up or you're going down.

Why, Lord, are You telling us this? We need to know why the Lord is telling us all this. "I have told you all this, so that your faith may not be shaken" (16:1). What does that have to do with it? Jesus told us all these things so that our faith would not be shaken. Do you realize how much your faith is shaken by the example of other people? Do you realize how much your faith depends on other human beings? Does your faith depend upon God and His witness, or the witness around you? How many people have left the Church because somebody is a hypocrite, or somebody is an adulterer and he goes to Mass every Sunday, or somebody embezzled, or somebody was a thief, or some priest hurt your feelings, or some nun slapped you across the room when you were in the sixth grade! All of those things have kept you from

God, kept you from Holy Mother Church, kept you from giving your life and committing your life to the Lord. So your faith was not built upon the witness of Jesus; it was built upon the witness of men, women, who are weak sinners like yourself.

Now just think. Perhaps a priest or a nun or a layman has been scandalous. So you lose your faith; you don't go to Mass anymore. You have this great, beautiful excuse: "I'm good. I don't need to go to Mass. I don't have to receive the sacraments. I don't kill. I don't murder. I don't do any of these things. I'm a good person." Maybe you're a good person. All you've been saying is what you're not doing to your neighbor. You have not even mentioned what you are doing to God. How can you say you love God when you never go to see Him? When you never receive that precious gift of the Eucharist into your heart, such a union that man could never have believed could exist? The union between a pure human sinner and His God. You're telling me that you love God and you refuse to accept the Eucharist on Sunday? You refuse to honor Him at Mass, and you say you love God? I find that impossible. When you know God, you want to go and say hi. Have you ever had a friend whom you never talk to? "Well, I talk to God at home." I'm glad you talk to Him sometimes, but I think you've got to visit Him and be fed with the Eucharist. You don't have to be "holy" or "good" to receive the Eucharist. You have to be in need. You have to say, "Jesus, I need You. Jesus, I want You."

We don't understand sometimes how we do ourselves so much harm by the bad example of other people. And I'm not saying you don't have good cause. I'm not saying that they were right or just. I'm not saying that they weren't evil in their actions. I am saying that you cannot allow the bad example of someone else to make you a bad example to someone else. You see, whatever occupies your mind and begins to possess it, you become the very thing you hate. It's important for you to understand that. You see, two evils don't help anything. So you are hurting yourself because someone else is hurting themselves. A person who is a hypocrite and goes to Mass, he's just piling up Purgatory and may lose his soul. The sister or priest who scandalized you or hurt you in any way, the Lord will take care of that. You can't hurt yourself. It's like stabbing yourself because somebody hurt you.

"They will expel you from the synagogue, and indeed the hour is coming, when anyone who kills you will think he's doing a holy duty for God" (16:2). We've got that in our own day and age. There's a tremendous persecution of the Catholic Church by terrible literature, sermons of ministers that are irate over the Church, and they think they're doing a duty to God. But the Lord says that's exactly what they're going to do. If there is anyone out there who is persecuting any denomination, listen to what the Lord is saying about you tonight. If you're persecuting someone, thinking you're doing a holy thing for God, the Lord said, "They will do these things because they have *never known* either the Father or myself" (16:3). Bishop Sheen said once that anyone who throws mud at another person loses his own ground.

"I have told you all this, so that ..." The Lord is preparing them for the hostile world. "So that when the time for it comes, you may remember that I told you" (16:4). Why are we so surprised when we're persecuted or people make fun of us because we know Jesus or speak of Jesus? Why are we so surprised? The Lord says, "I don't want you to be surprised. When your time comes, I want you to remember that I told you it would come." Now He says, "I did not tell you this from the outset, because I was with you" (16:4). If you've got Jesus, who cares? With Jesus walking by your side, who cares? With Jesus enlightening your mind, who cares? With Jesus standing tall before you, who cares? Nothing bothers you. So He says, "I was with you, you were protected. But now I'm going to the one who sent me. Not one of you has asked, 'Where are you going?' Yet you are sad at heart because I told you this" (see 16:5-6).

And then He says something that you and I, in our spiritual life, find hard to believe. He says, "I must tell you the truth: it is for your own good that I am going" (16:7). All of you that complain so much because you have a dry spell: the Lord seemed so near to you, and then suddenly He was far away. It seems like, for about a year, everything you asked the Lord for, He was Johnny-on-the-spot, and you had this nice warm feeling in your heart and everything was wonderful. And then you woke up one morning, and it was all gone. You didn't feel like praying. You didn't feel His presence. Virtue was hard; good habits just went down the drain; and nothing you asked for did you ever get. Everybody was bugging you. Everything seemed to be going downhill as fast as possible. And the Lord says, "It's for your good that I go." It really is.

Because you see, we all begin with faith, hope, and love at Baptism, as a little seed. Well, as you grow, it gets to be a bigger seed. As you get older and you begin to suffer and make the right decisions, it becomes a bigger seed. Now, we're talking about capacity. As you choose your God above yourself, this little seed becomes like a vessel. It's small, and it's all full of beautiful, beautiful, beautiful feelings. You know God and you're beginning to love the Scriptures. And it's just overflowing. It's just overflowing. And the Lord looks down and says, "That's too small. I want you to be big in the kingdom. I want you to have a lot of glory, a lot of honor, a lot of joy." So He stretches your soul. The grace of God stays in there, but now it kind of drops to the bottom, and you have all this empty space. It is a vacuum. In this little thing, you were filled, overflowing, but in this big one, it's just a tiny bit on the bottom. That's what dryness does. It takes this little vessel and widens it and makes it deeper.

Then, all of a sudden, you begin to make the right decisions again; you begin to love God with a pure love, and it begins to fill right back up again. And again, you think you've got it made, you've got the solution to holiness, and it's overflowing. And God says, "Well, it's still too small. I would like to make it *this* big." So you've got all this emptiness all over again. But you see what's happening? It gets bigger and bigger your whole life. That's why it's necessary sometimes that the Lord leaves you. He *never* leaves you. It just seems that way.

So He says, "I must tell you the truth: it's for your own good that I am going, because unless I go, the Advocate will not come to you" (16:7). Unless Jesus, with all His consolation and all the beauty of His life and all the joy, sometimes just seems to leave, the Spirit can't come. The Spirit is the builder. It's the Spirit's duty to make this little tiny vessel grow. You know, any time you remodel anything, it looks a mess. You've got boards everywhere, plaster coming down; it's dirty and messy, and the house looks terrible. But when it's finished, you've got two gorgeous rooms with new wallpaper, and you're so happy. But in order to get that, you have to tear down something old and something worn, like sin. We're talking about our body as a temple, the temple of our soul. It gets old sometimes; it gets worn out by sin and lack of virtue, so the Lord remodels. Now if you yell and kick and scream, and you want all this beauty and all this consolation and to feel good all the time, then you might stay stunted all your life. What a pity, if you force the Spirit to keep you from growing.

Well, how can I guarantee that I don't mess up the Spirit's work in myself? By living in the present moment. Some people think that during these dry spells and aridity and abandonment, they're losing their faith. No. Faith grows in aridity. Faith grows in dryness. Why? It's simple: because you're without feeling, you have to love God for Himself. Faith grows in darkness.

The Lord said, "You know, it's for your own good that I go, or the Advocate will not come to you. But if I go, I will send him to you." Earlier, in John 15:26, He said, "The Spirit of truth issues from the Father." Let me tell you what happens. There is tremendous love between Father and Son, so powerful, so infinite, so tremendous, that it is a Person. This Person issues forth from the Father and is sent by the Son, and so you have here the Trinity. Now, the Lord comes and goes in your life, by dryness, sufferings, anything at all, any heartache, tragedy, everything in life, joy, good things, everything. Every moment of your life, the Trinity resides in your heart, and what happens is that the love gets more and more intense, more intense, and as it gets more intense in your heart, it goes out to the world around you. And that's why Our Lord says, "It is necessary that I go. If I don't go, none of this will happen. You will not be able to love as the Father loves you. You will not be able to forgive your enemies or be merciful or compassionate or filled with hope or filled with faith. None of these will be possible until I begin to live my life in you and that life begins to penetrate your whole being."

A lot of things in your life happen that you just don't understand. Some of them don't make sense to you. Nothing here says they have to make sense. There's nothing here that says you have to understand. What the Lord wants you to do—through His Spirit, through that love constantly beating within your own heart—is to understand the joys and the love of the Spirit that come from faith in darkness, hope when you're discouraged, and love when it's difficult to love, in dryness.

All of that happens to you because Jesus sends the Spirit. And I must be attuned to that Spirit; I can't ignore Him. See, this is why

Jesus came. He came to save us, but I have to take the tools that He gave me, that He merited for me to possess. I would never possess these tools if He had not come and redeemed us. He gave me Baptism to clear my soul of Original Sin. He gave me the Eucharist so that my love, for Jesus and the Trinity and you, could grow and grow and grow, so He can love in me. He gave me Reconciliation, so when I sin, I can get rid of it. This is what Jesus merited. This is what the Spirit does. He is the Sanctifier. He comes with His seven gifts to build you up and make you holy in the same way that God is holy. So you are compassionate as God is compassionate. So you're holy as God is holy. And that is why Jesus came. That is what salvation means. It doesn't mean He went and paid your debt and now you're free. It means that when He paid your debt and He gave you all of these things, you have to take them, be grateful, and use them. They're talents in your hands.

Well, I hope you've enjoyed this fifth in the series on the spiritual life, and I hope you read these chapters and see what you get out of them. See if you can see God's economy and work in your life.

Praying in the Name of Jesus

We're going to continue with our secrets of holiness series by looking at the sixteenth chapter of John. Our dear Lord gave us the Word, the revelation of the Father's love, and the revelation of His death and Resurrection. He healed and He performed all the signs to prove He was the Messiah. And here in these chapters, He says, "Now, this is how you live the Christian life, how you live a deep interior life, where I make my home in you and you make your home in me." We're talking about a union with God that is very high and very exalted, and He puts it all in these chapters: John 14–17. These four chapters are filled with this spirituality that comes from Jesus Himself.

We left off at John 16:8. Jesus was talking about the Holy Spirit and saying, "If I don't go, He won't come." So the Spirit came because Jesus sent Him. He came to sanctify, to make us holy. So now He says, "When he comes, he will show the world how wrong it was" (16:8). How was the world wrong? The world is wrong by not accepting Jesus. He's going to convince the world, the world of Jesus' time and the world of our time, how wrong it was: "About sin, and about who was in the right, and about judgement" (16:8). The world's sin is its unbelief that Jesus is Lord and Son of God.

He explains: "About sin: proved by their refusal to believe in me" (16:9). So He explains that the sin of the world is the refusal.

Now, the word *refusal* is very interesting. Refusal to believe, which means they might have believed had they wanted to. We criticize them and say, "Oh, how terrible. Why did they not believe in Jesus?" Well, first of all, Jesus was not the kind of redeemer that they wanted. They wanted a political man. They wanted someone who would deliver them and be a military leader and bring them to the land of milk and honey once more. But are we sure we don't do something similar to that? Is Jesus the kind of redeemer we want? Is the suffering Jesus in this generation the kind of redeemer we want? Or are we not always trying to make Jesus out to be the person who makes you healthy, wealthy, and wise, and that Christianity brings you all the good things of life? Do we want a suffering redeemer? Are we really better than those who rejected Him?

You see, we have to ask ourselves some pretty tough questions here, because we criticize these people for not accepting Jesus. But we have to know *why* they didn't accept Jesus. And sometimes, you know, we don't accept Jesus either. In atheistic countries, they have the Cross without Jesus. And I'm wondering if sometimes in Christian countries, we don't have Jesus without the Cross. Jesus is *on* the Cross. Yes, I understand He resurrected, but it's just as much a scandal today as it was in the day of Paul. It's a scandal, all the suffering in my life and your life. Our personal suffering sometimes scandalizes us. Sometimes we say, "Jesus, I'm doing all I can. I'm keeping Your commandments. I'm doing everything possible to live a good life, and yet all these terrible things come upon me." Is that not a scandal sometimes to us? Do we really want a suffering redeemer? Do we really want to imitate a suffering redeemer? I don't question that it's hard. I find it hard. You find it hard. It doesn't matter how hard we find it, as long as we accept it.

He goes on: "About who was in the right: proved by my going to the Father and your seeing me no more" (16:10). What He is saying is that the Spirit will demonstrate to the world that Jesus has a *right* to the title of Son of God, and that His passing from this world, His death, would lead Him to His home. "I'm going to the Father," He said. That's home. And the Spirit would have to plant that into men's hearts. He says, "The Spirit is going to convince the world about judgment, proved by the prince of this world being already condemned" (16:11). In other words, the death of Jesus would permanently condemn the enemy of God, who is your enemy too. Jesus redeemed us; He brought us up from our misery to the Father's love.

And then He goes on to say, "I still have many things to say to you, but they would be too much for you now" (16:12). You know, that's an interesting sentence. You and I sometimes wonder why God doesn't tell us things and why He doesn't answer all our prayers. Well, you know what, I just witnessed something this past week. Someone prayed and prayed and prayed and prayed for something, and we prayed with them. Well, they got what they prayed for and started going all the way down. I wonder if it wouldn't have been better if he hadn't had those prayers answered. Only God knows the end result, but I'm convinced that sometimes you and I don't get our prayers answered because we might lose our souls. Could we handle what we're asking for? I'm more convinced of it today than I ever was in my life that it's best for us to just trust the Lord. After we have asked for something, and if He doesn't give it to us, trust Him, because He knows best. Some things are just too much for us to have or to know.

There comes a point in our life where we think we know, but we don't. Sometimes we wonder if it is wise to ask for anything? Yeah, we should ask. But what I'm saying is that sometimes I don't think the things we ask for are for our good, and God knows that.

The wisdom we should have in asking for things is a little bit self-oriented, not geared toward asking: *Is this the will of God? Is this going to be for my eternal salvation?* Is what I'm asking for my eternal salvation? Am I ready to receive what I'm asking for? If I'm asking for eternal salvation, sure. Eternal salvation is something that may be now, may be tomorrow. You know, when we talk about salvation, you think it's always way out in the distance. I can't help the last few days thinking about all those elderly people going home from Reno, Nevada, and suddenly the bus is going too fast or whatever the reason was, but it veered off the road and went into a ravine. So many of them were killed in ice-cold water. Unbelievable. A quick, sudden death. So, as we ask for so many things in life, we must always remember that we first of all don't know how long life is for us. And secondly, we're not too sure it's for our good. We only think so.

Let's go on. He says, "When the Spirit of truth comes, he will lead you to the complete truth" (16:13). Complete truth. Not half-truths. He will let you know that Jesus is really and truly Son of God. That's a gift of faith. The Spirit gives it to you, and if you don't have it, ask for it. I've heard people say, "Mother, I don't have any faith." The fact that you even know you don't have faith is to already desire it. "I wish I had faith." To say "I wish I had faith" is the beginning of faith. The Spirit places the desire in your heart. You can't wish for faith without the Spirit. So if you wish you had faith or had more faith, then you already are on the way because only the Spirit places within your heart the desire for more faith. So often in the spiritual life, we already possess, at least in seed form, the very thing we're asking for. And that comes as a surprise, but it's true. Let's go on.

Now, you know, here's one more of those places in Scripture that are so phenomenal. Talking about the Spirit of truth, Jesus says, "He will not be speaking as from himself but will say only what he has learnt" (16:13). Everything comes from the Father. The Word, the Word who was made flesh, Jesus, said over and over, "I only say what I hear from the Father. I only do what I see the Father do." So the Spirit, too, will not be saying anything from Himself but will only say what He has learned from the Father. Everything comes from the Father. Jesus is the perfect knowledge the Father has of Himself. And the Spirit is that love. They are three different Persons but only one God. Only one God. And that's why Jesus is saying here that the Spirit will get everything from the Father and give to you. And the Son gives to you what He gets from the Father. And so we all tend toward the Father.

This is what the Spirit does: "He will glorify me, since all he tells you will be taken from what is mine. Everything the Father has is mine; that is why I said: All he tells you will be taken from what is mine" (16:14-15). Jesus gets everything from the Father; the Spirit gets everything from the Father. We have Love, Word, and Father. Three persons. Only one God. So all the source of truth is from one source. And that's why Jesus can say, "Everything the Father has is mine." Everything the Spirit has is from Jesus, and everything Jesus has is from the Father.

Now, this is a very important aspect of our spiritual life, because you and I are to do exactly the same thing. You find Jesus always giving credit to the Father for everything He said and did. And now He's saying that the Spirit will not be giving what's from Himself but what belongs to Jesus, and Jesus will get it from the Father. "Everything the Father has is mine. Everything the Spirit will take is from me. Everything I have is from the Father." So we're always going back, back, back to the Father. And for you and me, as we prepare our souls, as we prepare ourselves to give our souls back to God at a certain time that we call death, this is what should happen.

Remember, you have three faculties. You have a memory, and you have an intellect, and you have a will. This soul is made up of three distinct faculties. They're all different, but still, you have only one soul. So now, when you're baptized, the Spirit comes and places the Father in your memory; He places the Son in your intellect; and He places Himself in your will. So you've got this memory, the "heart" that Jesus refers to. The Father should be the main instrument within this faculty, so that when things happen to you, you can forgive, you can prevent yourself from getting angry to the point of hatred, you can prevent resentment, an unforgiving spirit, selfishness, egotistical attitudes. And so you want to be compassionate. Jesus said, "Be compassionate as your Father is compassionate" (Luke 6:36). So I know that if I am compassionate and merciful, my memory will always be like the Father.

And then, my reason will act accordingly. That's what's wrong with the world—one of the things wrong with the world today—it is losing so quickly the sense of compassion and of mercy. We live in a violent, fearful society. You feel it when you read a paper, when you hear the news. It's all around us. This memory is being filled with pornography and immorality and lack of values. Everything is being pushed into this memory, and so it's harder and harder for us to keep the Father there, to keep the words of Scripture there, to keep goodness and compassion and mercy. You keep fighting all day long. Some people, it seems right to hate them. Some incidents and events, it seems right to lash out. So we have excuses that we use, in the name of truth, for hating, for being resentful, for harboring anger and all these things. We keep pushing garbage into our memory, so we don't hear the Father, and we can no longer say, "I only do what I see the Father do. I only say what I hear the Father say."

The Father wants me to be compassionate; he wants me to be merciful. So often, I don't think with a humble heart; I think with a proud heart. When Jesus came, He merited for me to be humble—humble of heart. See, if I'm humble of heart, knowing that I can admit my fault without going to pieces, that I can see myself and arrive at self-knowledge without falling apart, then I can take it if my neighbor says, "Why do you get so angry? Why are you impatient? Why did you act this way, why did you act that way?" I can say, "I don't know, I'm sorry." But if I'm going to fight against that knowledge ... Many times, sure, you can justify your actions. But is it holy justification, or is it selfishness?

And the Spirit is love. So you see, I've got the Trinity in me, and I must do in my spiritual life exactly what the Spirit and Jesus do: give all the acknowledgment to the Father. So if I develop compassion and mercy, I could make giant strides in holiness.

Let's go on now. Jesus says, "In a short time, you will no longer see me, and then a short time later you will see me again" (16:16). And here He refers, of course, to His Resurrection, the glory that is to come. Now, for those of you who say you don't understand the Scriptures, that they are too hard, here's another point where you and I can get a little courage. Remember that the Lord told these apostles many times during His lifetime that He was going to go to Jerusalem, that He would be mocked, scourged, crowned with thorns, and would die, but on the third day be raised. He told them three, four times. Well, it didn't dawn on them. Because here again they're saying, "What does He mean?" Some of His disciples said to one another, "What does he mean, 'In a short time you will no longer see me, and then a short time later you will see me again' and, 'I am going to the Father'? What is this 'short time'? We don't know what he means" (16:17–18). Now, you talk about being dense.

Well, Our Lord, always knowing what their thoughts were, said, "You are asking one another what I meant.... I tell you most solemnly, you will be weeping and wailing while the world will rejoice" (16:19-20). We all know that during the Crucifixion and during the trial, there were many people rejoicing, thinking, "Oh, we're gonna get rid of this man, this troublemaker." Meanwhile, the apostles were weeping and wailing. There are many of us who suffer unjustly, while those who try to do us in rejoice, thinking they've really hit us hard this time. And yet He says, "You will be sorrowful, but your sorrow will turn to joy" (16:20). Our Lord is saying that to each one of us, "You will weep, you will wail, you will be sorrowful, you will cry, but your sorrow will be turned into joy." That is hope. We can stand tall on the hope that Jesus has given us. He will not go down on His promises. He will not forget what He told us. He promised us that, for all our tears and our anxiety and frustration and heartache, there will be joy.

Now He wants to give us a comparison. He wants to explain the difference between that ultimate pain and the ultimate joy, so that we look forward, past the present moment. No matter what I'm going through today, I can look beyond it. That's the hope of the Christian. He says, "A woman in childbirth suffers because her time has come, but when she has given birth to the child she forgets the suffering in her joy that a man has been born into the world" (16:21). The Lord is making a comparison. And you and I have had that experience many, many times. For example, when you're good and healthy, you can't imagine yourself being sick. And there are times when you're sick, you can't imagine yourself being healthy.

There are many joys in life—although some people are born in pain and die in pain—but for most people, there is a combination. It isn't that you're *paying* for happiness; it isn't like you're buying it. In other words, it isn't that the Lord is saying, "Oh, you're happy today; I'm gonna make you miserable tomorrow." Or, "You're miserable now; I'll make you happy tomorrow." No. We live in an imperfect situation, in an imperfect way, in an imperfect world, and we are the victims of other people's imperfections. So there is no way, in this life, that you can have happiness all the time. Your own nature changes from day to day. If you feel great one day, the next day you feel tired, and you don't even know why you feel tired. There is a combination in this world of pain, sorrow, and joy. However, He says here, "You are sad now, but I shall see you again, and your hearts will be full of joy, and *that* joy no one shall take from you" (16:22).

So what is the joy that Jesus promised that no one would take from us? I don't know about you, but I know a lot of things can happen in my life that take joy away from me. If I don't have enough money to pay our debts, and I see everything starting to go downhill, my joy is a little bit crimped. And we're all that way. So what is the bottom-line joy that Jesus said no one can take from us? St. Paul said it one time: "What shall separate me from the love of Christ? Persecution or suffering or pain?" And in the end, he said, "Nothing shall" (see Rom. 8:35–39). The joy that Jesus is talking about is the joy of knowing, first of all, that, no matter what happens, you are loved by God and that you are going home to Him. And then, in comparison, everything in this life fades. It is nothing in comparison to the joy of knowing that I'm loved by God, I am cared for by God, and He knows me by name. And one day I shall be happy with Him in the kingdom. He redeemed me. Now, *that* kind of joy can be laced between every other pain and sorrow, just like a fine silk thread, and it gives us, in the midst of a war—war within and the war without—peace.

Every day, the Lord gives us that special kind of joy that is laced between everything in life—the sorrows as well as the joys of life that we call happiness. In between, there is always a serenity, that, in the midst of the most exalted thing in our life, we can always think of Jesus, thank Him, thank Him that we have the Father in our minds and hearts. And that's so important, so that we're not always up and down like an elevator. How do you arrive at that serenity of soul? Some people go up, and they stay up for a while; then they come down—*boom*. And why is that? What happens is that so often we expect things and people to be the same way. It's so important that you understand that God loves you, so that your life, although it does have its ups and downs, is a kind of gentle curve.

First, God loves me. That is most important. You might ask, "Isn't it more important that we love one another?" You can't love everybody unless you know God loves you. You have to have love within you. Supernatural love within me makes me love you. If you only love in a natural way, how many people can you love? You're going to love the people you like. So how many people do you like? Well, your family. Maybe there's a few in your family you don't like. So how many people are you going to like? If you're only going to love the people you like, then there's not gonna be that many people. But I've got to be like God. I have to love like God. I can't do that unless I have an awful lot of love to give. If I love only on my own, I have only a little love to give, so I'm gonna love this one and this one and this one, but I'm not gonna love everybody. I'm only going to love a few. But when I love God and I know God loves me, then I can love everyone, even my enemies.

Maybe you don't want to love your enemy. What does it mean, to love my enemy? It means you pray for them, you wish them well, and if you had the opportunity, you would do something nice for them. You say, "Are you sure this is pure love, if I love him just because God wants me to and I don't feel like it?" Yes, because you're obeying the command of God, and you're not hating like maybe your nature would like you to do; you're loving instead, which means you've made a choice in favor of God and against your own human inclinations.

Our Lord goes on to say, "When that day comes, you will not ask me any questions. I tell you most solemnly, anything you ask for from the Father he will grant in my name" (16:23). He will grant in my name. Anything. You could say, "Well, I can think of a lot of things I asked for in the name of Jesus, and I didn't get it." Remember above where He said, "Ask and you shall receive, so your joy will be complete." What do I ask God for? There are things we ask for that are not for our good. Do you think God's going to give them to you? I don't. I wouldn't give you something that you asked me for if I thought it was not for your good. When your children want to play with matches, you don't give them matches. The child doesn't know why. "Why can't I play with matches?" "Because you're gonna get burned." "I don't mind getting burned." "Yes, you will." So the motive behind your prayer is extremely important. Whatever you ask for, and I don't even care if you're asking for a parking place, the motive has to be for your good. You must ask God only for what is for your good. Not what you *think* is for your good, but what God knows is for your good. And then you will always get the right answer from God. You always get the right answer, because the Lord is not going to give you something that is not for your good. He loves you too much.

Sometimes we can create a situation in which we pray for something, but God isn't quite real to us, and we don't have this confidence the Lord is talking about. We pray but we say, "Well, is He there or not?" There's where you need to say, "Jesus, Lord, Father, I know You're there. I'm having a hard time today with my faith. I'm having a hard time even believing You know me or

You love me or You even exist. But Lord, I pour out my heart to You." Be honest with God. If you can't be honest with God, who are you gonna be honest with?

And that's the joy that our Lord is talking about here where He says your joy will be complete. Once you have just poured out your soul to the Lord, you know for sure, just as the Lord knew, that He only did what He knew the Father wanted Him to do. So when you ask in His name, you're going to ask the way Jesus asked: "Father, I only do what I see you do, and I only say what I hear you say." You're gonna do the same: "Father, I only ask for what You want me to ask, and if I'm not asking for what You want me to ask You, I don't want it." That's got to be the purest prayer in the world. So if you can be at peace with that prayer, you've got joy that never, never ends. It takes a lot of unselfishness, doesn't it? But you've got the Trinity living within you to give you the power to pray that pure prayer: "Father, I ask for this in your Son's holy name, but I pray as your Son prayed. I only want what You want for me. If what I'm asking is not what You want for me, I don't want it." You'll never miss with that prayer.

Let's go on. The Lord says, "I've been telling you all this in metaphors, but the hour is coming when I shall no longer speak to you in metaphors" (16:25). He kind of cloaked His whole messianic message. Although He healed and delivered and spoke very bluntly sometimes in the temple and to the apostles at night He explained things, there were always parables, metaphors. But now He says, "You're gonna get real life. The Spirit is going to come upon you and you're going to see things in a whole new way and you're going to see them as they are, because you're gonna have the power of the Spirit to be able to accept them. You're going to have the power of the Spirit in order to take it. You're going to have the power and the guts to live what I've asked you to live."

We see here how Jesus says to us exactly the same thing over and over in a different way. "When that day comes you will ask in my name"—the name of Jesus—"and I do not say that I shall pray to the Father for you" (16:26). Here we're gonna make a great leap. Jesus is telling us: "When you pray, I do not say I shall pray to the Father for you, because the Father himself loves you for loving me and believing that I came from God" (16:26-27). In other words, faith is so powerful that it goes to the Father like an arrow, so that when you love Jesus, when you believe in Jesus, the Father loves you because you believe in Jesus, because you believe that He is the Son of God.

And we don't have to worry about *how much* we believe and what degree of belief we have. Don't categorize yourself in some little box; don't put yourself in a corner and then brick yourself up. You don't know. You can't decide what degree of love you have for God. Only God knows that. But if you believe and you love Jesus, He says, "I don't even have to intercede for you because the Father himself loves you for loving me." The Father, in other words, hears your prayer immediately. This is a tremendous thing to know. Now, I bet most of you out there don't even believe God hears you or loves you. But Jesus is saying, "Because you love me, because you believe what I say, because your hope is founded in my word, the Father loves you and you can pray to the Father." I mean, this is why Jesus came, that you and I might go to the Father. We have something very special.

You might say, "How come then you pray to saints? How come you pray to Mary?" Because they also pray to the Father for me. Jesus never said I shouldn't ask others to pray to the Father. "Where there are two or more gathered in my name, I am in the midst" (see Matt. 18:20). So if I can pray with you or with St. Anthony, it's the same thing. If there are two of us. And believe me, I'd rather have Our Lady on my side than anybody else. We all go to the Father because of Jesus.

We've gone through a lot of things, but the most important, I think, is the fact that you and I have a Father in Heaven, the Father of Jesus, your Father and my Father. And because we believe in Jesus, because we believe He is Lord, the Father hears our prayer. We have other advocates in Heaven. We call them saints; we call one the Mother of God. And all together, we cry out, because through Jesus, through the power of the Spirit, we can say, "Abba, Father." And in that, we can be content that whether our prayers are answered or not, according to our way of thinking, they're always answered in the wisdom of God. We can be assured of His love and of the peace we receive from the reality of having the joy that no one can take away from us, because it is rooted in the holy will of God that is within us and around us in the present moment.

So let us rejoice that we have been called to believe in Jesus, to praise Him, and to proclaim His holy name. Wherever you go, at least once a day, why don't you try to tell someone about Jesus, about the good news that we have a Father in Heaven and that He is our Father, because we have Jesus as Lord and Savior. I love you, and God loves you so much that nobody could ever describe it, so take courage in that and be at peace. For you and I are dear to God. And although we don't feel it sometimes, we are. So rejoice in your dignity as a child of God, and tell Him often how much you love Him.

The Peace of Jesus

We have been looking at St. John's Gospel. In John 14–17 we have the entire blueprint for the interior spiritual life.

You might say, "Well, why do I need an interior life? There are so many real things happening."

What is *real*? I would say that a thing that you can tear up and destroy is not real, because it ceases to exist. This table — I can burn it, and it would be just a little handful of ashes. So many of the things we call real are only temporary. They're all temporary. Even our coastline is changing. Everything is passing. So when you say: "I'm in the *real* world …"

Now, if you say, "I'm in the world," meaning you're miserable, oh yeah, I can buy that. But is that the real world? I mean, the drunkenness and orgies, debauchery, and all the other things that man is capable of and is doing in this day and age, murdering the innocent and killing the old, all in the name of mercy, protected by law. And we call that real. It's unbelievable what you and I call real.

"Well, Mother, you know, God made me in this world, and I've got to eat and sleep and drink, and I gotta handle the things of the world." Oh sure, I buy that. I have to do that too. But that's what we have to *do*.

I don't question that all the things happening are real. They hurt. When something hurts me, it's real. But if I totally ignore the *other* reality, that permits me to endure in the midst of chaos, in the midst of all the things that we fight with and fight for and fight against—I cannot possibly endure all those things with any kind of sanity unless I am in the *real* world, the *world of God*. You see, most of the things happening today in our world don't make sense. They just don't make sense. You see our youngsters just wasting their life away; they're dissipated and sophisticated by the time they're ten or twelve years old. You see them walking down the street, all made up, no more than thirteen or fourteen, smoking cigarettes. They're already on the way out.

A friend of mine said something so sad to me, not too long ago. He was in New York. Even those who practice sin have levels and degrees, so the good hookers and prostitutes are in one section of the city, and, as they become more and more useless and dissipated, they go down into the lower parts of the city. What misery. And in the lower part of New York, where has-been prostitutes would be, those who have been in the business and are worn out and no longer attractive to anybody, in that section was a fourteen-year-old kid. We call that the real world. You gotta ask yourself, "What have we done to God's world?" Where is it going? And why don't we change it? It only takes one person: the Lord Jesus. You and I must be determined to be holy as God is holy.

So the apostles say to Jesus, "What do you mean that you're gonna go away for a short time and we won't see you, and then you're coming back and we'll see you? We don't understand that" (see John 16:17–18). If you don't understand the Scriptures, don't feel bad. The apostles didn't understand even though they had Jesus standing right in front of them. So the Lord explains, "I came from the Father and have come into the world and now I leave the world to go to the Father" (16:28). He didn't say "I die" but "I leave the world." The only time the Lord uses the word *die* is when someone loses his soul. Every other time, He talks about death as sleep, a transition. On October 4, when St. Francis died, we have a little ceremony called the *transitus*, the transition of Francis from this world to the other. That's one of the greatest needs we have today: remembering the other world and remembering that this world is only a preparation for the next.

And so the Lord knew that His work was about finished and He was leaving this world and going back to the Father. Then the apostles say, "Now you are speaking plainly and not using metaphors! Now we see that you know everything and do not have to wait for questions to be put into words; because of this we believe you came from God" (16:29-30). Do you have questions you've never put into words? I know I do. I suppose we all do in a way, but I think the more you ask, the more you learn.

So Our Lord is kind of astounded at these apostles. You know, we think our Lord was just so out of this world because of His divinity that He didn't feel all the anxieties, the frustrations of life. I guess the greatest frustration was that the men He was teaching to lead His Church hardly ever understood what He said. All you parents out there who are so unhappy because your kids never understand what you say—Our Lord had the same kind of experience.

"Do you believe at last?" He says (16:31). "Finally, I'm on my way home, and now you believe." We wait until our bones creak before we finally get the message: I was created for God, by God, and to be with God. Isn't it a shame? It takes all our life before we finally get to that knowledge.

Well, the Lord wants them to know something: "The time has come—in fact it has already come—when you will be scattered, each going his own way and leaving me alone" (16:32). Just when they thought they had the message and they were beginning to understand, the Lord socks them with this one: "You're going to scatter and leave me alone." That's the saddest sentence in Scripture. The Lord Jesus, the Eternal Word, the Word come down from the bosom of the Father, who came down and lived among us—what an awesome gift for all of us—was left alone because all His friends split. All of you that are lonely—a lot of you that listen to this program in apartment houses, convalescent homes, in your own home; your husband died; your children are gone; you talk to the walls; the only voice outside of your own is either the dog or the cat or the radio and television—you're not alone, no more than He was alone. Because that's exactly what He says in the next sentence. And I know it's hard. I know you say, "I want someone with skin on to talk to. I don't wanna have to imagine God is with me." But you don't need to *imagine* He is with you. He is. He *is* with you. And this is what our Lord is saying. It is so sad and yet so awesomely beautiful. He says, "And yet I am not alone, because the Father is with me" (16:32).

Now, when we say we're alone or we're lonely, what are we talking about? We're talking about the absence of other creatures, that's all. The absence of other creatures is what makes us lonely; so it's an absence, it's very negative. But the Lord says, "You, my friends, you're gonna go. You're gonna be scattered and leave me alone. But I'm not alone. The Father's with me." In these few little sentences is the essence of the entire life inside of you, which we call the interior life. We have to be realistic: if you're by yourself in the house, you're by yourself in the house; you can't imagine there's twenty people there. But in the absence of people, there is a presence so awesome that you have to be attuned to it and acknowledge it, just like you have to acknowledge people in your house. Now, some men never acknowledge the presence of their wife, and they sit right there eating a meal she worked all afternoon to make. You can have twenty people in the house and still be alone if no one's talking to you or you don't really care for each other and really love each other. So it isn't not having people around that makes you alone; you're alone inside. But an aloneness inside must be a presence, one that you have to acknowledge, love, talk to, and understand.

You know, when I get frustrated, and that's often, and everything seems to be coming in on me—I mean everything just seems to be getting closer and closer and closer; there's more and more and more demand and less and less time—when I begin to feel myself going into an igloo, I just stop and become aware of that awesome presence of God, which all these things have shoved out for a few moments or hours. And suddenly it's like something lifts. It's no longer burdensome, and it's no longer a pain; it's no longer a sacrifice. It's a presence. And if you really want to be able to bear your burdens—and some of you have real heavy burdens, there's just no question of it—you've got to be very aware of His presence and that you're never alone. For just a minute, I want you to close your eyes and just shut yourself out from everything around you and be aware of that presence.

Now, this next verse kind of explains a lot. In those moments when you just feel hemmed in, when you're disappointed, you're disgruntled, go within yourself. If you're in your home alone, or you can go and sit in your car a moment with your eyes closed—the car parked, of course—go within yourself and begin to make yourself aware of this presence around you. Listen to the silence. Shut off your radio; shut out the noise for a few minutes. Listen to the silence and know that you're in tune with the presence of God.

And the Lord says here, "I have told you all this so that you may find peace in me" (16:33). I can find peace in Jesus by imitating

Him, by doing the very thing He did. The only way I can find peace in my heart is to take His words and His example and apply them to my life. The Bible is not some magic book that you recite a few words of and suddenly a lot of things happen within you. This is for imitation, not just emulation. *Imitation.* You're not just to admire the Scriptures or Jesus; you've got to take them into yourself and make Him a part of your whole life. Your whole life. That is the purpose. That is why you have this book. That's what you need to do.

Now, some of you may be saying, "Well, Mother, that's nice, to know what Jesus did. It is nice to know He wants me to do it, but when I was meditating just now during the break, I didn't feel His presence." Well, we're not talking about feeling anything; we're not talking about having goose bumps and these little things going up and down your spine. We're talking about the reality and the acceptance of reality. If you're going to go by your feelings, you're going to go up and down like a yo-yo. Faith is in tune with reality, and the reality is that He is present.

Those of you who've been married ten, fifteen, twenty years, even if you've had a good marriage, your love isn't as effervescent as it was in the beginning. You say, "Isn't that terrible?" No, it's not terrible. Love gets deeper, and you begin to be content with presence. You don't have to do as many things to make each other aware that you love each other; you're totally convinced. After years of suffering together, sometimes arguing, sometimes quarreling, overcoming all these things, love grows deeper and deeper and deeper, and you are content to be in each other's presence; you don't need the goose bumps. That's how it is with God. You don't need to feel. That's where faith comes in. I want to get you away from using faith like a nickel in a slot machine, and you pull the thing and then, all of a sudden, God pours down all these graces.

Faith is something real, meaning I am convinced of the Word of God; I am convinced of His presence; and I live by that, whether or not my prayers are answered. They're *my* prayers. I can't say I always ask for the right thing, that I always ask for what's good for me.

Now He says, "In the world, you will have trouble, but be brave: I have conquered the world" (16:33). Now you say, "Great. *You've* conquered the world. What's it mean to me? I obviously have not conquered the world." If you're an alcoholic and you're on drugs, or you're over-sexed, obviously the *world* has conquered *you*; you haven't conquered the world. The world pulls you around; the world has a ring in your nose and pulls and pushes you where it wants. Society does. Somebody God-knows-where decides what you wear; they decide what your hairdo looks like; and we just follow like cattle. You have to understand that the world has conquered today. And yet Jesus says, "Be brave. Don't be afraid. I have conquered the world." Which means the grace that He has merited for you and for me is so powerful that we don't have to say *yes* to everything. We can say *no*. We can live a holy life.

So when you're lonely, you have a choice. Are you just gonna go to pot, or are you going to become aware? Are you going to *react*, or are you going to *respond* to that presence of God? Are you going to react to the absence of people or respond to the living presence around you, within you? And that is what the Lord is trying to say in these two sentences. He's saying, "Respond; don't react. I have overcome the world. You need not worry about all the pressures in the world. I have overcome. I have conquered the world. Be brave."

You see, the fact that He conquered gives you, gives me, the grace. We have the Spirit within us. That's why Baptism is so important today. I have the Spirit within me that makes me solid, unafraid of the pressures of life. People crack up because they become fearful, and so the pressures, life, the world, they begin to take possession and dictate exactly how you're going to feel, how you're going to act, how you're going to think. And as a result, we're reeds shaken in the wind by every kind of doctrine and every kind of theology and every kind of pressure. But the Lord did not live and die and rise from the dead for us to be reeds shaken by the wind. You see, He has given us His very self; that's what the Spirit is. The Spirit is love. God is love. So every one of us has this within us, if we pray, if we're aware of His presence, and there we find peace in the midst of chaos. Not peace in the *absence* of turmoil or the *absence* of chaos. Life in the world *is* chaos. The physical world is beautiful, but when man leaves God, when our laws are such that we can murder and kill, we get to be like another Sodom and Gomorrah. We get to a point where we don't sense evil or sense sin because we're so in the midst of it. And the Lord said, "Don't be afraid. Be brave. Stand tall. I have overcome the world. I give you my presence. In the Eucharist, I give you my Body, my Blood, my Soul, my Divinity. I come and live with you. You have me in you. It's the two of us together."

And this is what He says: "Father, the hour has come: glorify your Son so that your Son may glorify you" (17:1). What in the world is He talking about? He is about to be terribly mutilated, be crucified, and die. How is that going to glorify the Father? How do your sufferings and your heartaches glorify God? The same way His did. By making you strong, by making you exercise faith and hope and love and building your soul so that you become the image of Jesus.

And He says, "Through the power over all mankind that you have given him, let him give eternal life to all those you have entrusted to him" (17:2). When you're able to accept the suffering in your life, you give eternal life to all the people around you. Why? Because they are edified, and they begin to know there is something more to life than they're getting. Your life is an example of the presence of God. Because you are able to accept the same kind of sufferings that Jesus went through His entire life as they are put upon your shoulders, when His burden and your burden become one burden, then the whole world will know. That's what He said earlier on, "I give you a new commandment. By the love you have for one another, all men will know I was sent by the Father." They will know that there is a Jesus, there is a Messiah, there is a Christ, there is a Savior, because the world cannot give you peace in the midst of turmoil. It only gives you more anxiety, more frustration.

And He goes on: "And eternal life is this" (17:3). What is eternal life? The answer is given to us by Jesus Himself: "To know you, the only true God, and Jesus Christ whom you have sent." That is eternal life. And it's got to begin here and now. Some people think they're just gonna live it up and when they die, all of a sudden, *whoom*, they're up in the eternal Heaven glorifying God. If you haven't glorified God here, if you haven't even had a desire ...

Now, I'm not talking about feelings. If you're sick, if you have any kind of chronic disease or terminal disease, you don't *feel* like praying—your body is racked with pain—any more than Jesus did. But when Jesus was on the Cross, that is when He glorified the Father in a very special way. So those of you that are sick and can't go to Mass, you *are* a Mass. Your body is the altar; your pain is the sacrifice. If you're in bed and you can't go to Mass, you can go to Communion; someone will bring you Communion, and you need that at least once a week, if not more. You need that Real Presence within you, in order to endure *your Mass*, your sacrifice. There's where you glorify the Father the same way Jesus did. When you can believe and know the one true God and Jesus, His Son, in a body that's racked with pain and distress and heartache and suffering of every kind, you are glorifying the Father. The world may not understand. But the world never will.

And He goes on and says, "I have glorified you on earth"—he's talking to the Father—"and finished the work you gave me to do" (17:4). As you and I get older in life, we will all one day say, "I have finished the work you gave me to do." What is the work? Jesus' work was the salvation of mankind. Your work is the salvation of your soul. Jesus paid the price. He paid it once for all. The Mass, as we have it every morning, is not another death, but the one and only, that you and I have the privilege to be present at. That sacrifice is yours.

The work you have been given to do ... Some might say, "I don't know, I haven't been given anything to do." If you say that, you are thinking like the world does, because your idea of having something to do is to have glory, to be some kind of celebrity, or to have all the world applaud you, to have some high office and lots of money. That's the world. You have a mission. You may not know it until you reach that beautiful moment we call death. And then you will know. You'll say, "I didn't know all that happened because of me: all these souls were saved because I was so lonely in an apartment and I gave it to you, Lord; all those children were saved, Lord, because I offered this pain for love of You." This isn't just being pietistic. It's basic fact; it's reality. We've got to live by the reality that is everlasting.

Now He says, "Now, Father, it is time for you to glorify me" (17:5). He keeps saying it because He has understood the power of suffering. In today's world, we have long forgotten the power of suffering. We don't even want to hear about it, and so we cover it up with flowery speech, and we make it out to be an evil that we need to be healed of. But the Lord says, "Glorify me with that glory I had with you before ever the world was" (17:5). He's going back; His work is about to be finished; but the greatest work was the redemption of mankind, and He did that through pain.

I have a hard time figuring out how some of you think you're above that pain, and you're above that suffering. We expect redemption to treat us like spoiled children. We want a Cadillac in every garage, a chicken in every pot, and everything hunky-dory. I call that unrealistic—really unrealistic. Because when Jesus said that He is glorifying the Father through His pain, you are doing the same thing. I'm not saying you shouldn't take an aspirin or go to doctors. I send my sisters to doctors, and I take whatever medication the doctor gives me, but there are some pains in life—and you know what I'm talking about—that medication will never take away. Never take away. And you and I have to endure.

He says, "I have made your name known" (17:6). Isn't that wonderful? If you and I could say the same: "Father, I have finished the work you have given me to do. I have made your name known to the men that you took from the world to give me" (17:4, 6). If we could say: "I've made Your name known to the family that you have given me, to the people, the friends, the relatives, the neighbors, my coworkers. I have glorified Your name to all of these people. I have done the work You've given me to do. And now I come home."

"They were yours"—these men that had been chosen by the Father—"they were yours and you gave them to me" (17:6). You know, it's amazing to me how Jesus attributes every single thing He does or says to the Father. He says, "These men were yours. You gave them to me." You and I would have said, "I wanna thank You, Father, for the men I have chosen, or the men You have given me to choose." We would have put ourselves in there somehow. But Jesus is so much alive in the Father, from whence He comes. You and I come from God. If we realized that, there would be no abortion today. There would be no abortion. We have taken away God's sovereign rights. And Jesus is so, so different.

He says, "Now at last they know that all you have given me comes indeed from you" (17:7). He just can't stop pointing everything back to the Father. "They know now that everything you have given me really, truly comes from you." That's all He wanted the apostles to know: that He came from the Father, that it was the Father who sent Him, that it was the Father who did the works He was doing, that it was the Father who was speaking the words He was speaking. And He says, "Now at last they know ... for I have given them the teaching you gave to me" (17:7-8). The humility of Jesus is so profound that you and I miss it. If I were to say a prayer on the air and say, "Father, I thank You for the words You have given me," some of you would be scandalized and say, "Oh, Mother, what makes you think that the Father gave you these words?" Because I know they're not mine. So, whether you believe it or not, it would be true.

All of you who have some exterior talent, like artists, writers, doctors, lawyers, physicians, surgeons—all of that has been given to you by the Father. And when you appropriate it to yourself alone as if it was initiated by you and came directly from your own mind, without any outside gift, then you alienate yourself from the Giver of all life. We call that pride. And Jesus, over and over, says, "I have given them the teaching you gave me." He wasn't witnessing to Himself; He only witnessed to the Father. Isn't that absolutely phenomenal? Do you and I do that? You say, "Well, wait a minute. If I make a cherry pie tomorrow, am I supposed to say to my husband, 'The Lord made this cherry pie'?" No. But you should say, "Praise God for this cherry pie."

Have you ever been so sick that you thought you'd never be well again? I had an operation one time, and I remember lying in that bed for days, and you know, I could not imagine myself having the strength to walk out of that room. It seemed like I would never walk again, that I would never feel good again. That's the way we are. And so, our dear Lord wants us to know that all the strength we have, that we take for granted—the eyes that see, the ears that hear—are all gifts from God. And if they're taken away, He gives us something better. Those that are blind hear what we do not hear. And those that are deaf see what we do not see. God is always giving and giving.

And He said, "They have truly accepted this, that I came from you, and have believed that it was you who sent me" (17:8). That's all He wanted. He just wanted to bear witness to the truth. And the truth is that God is Father and Jesus is His Son. That's the truth. It's all He wanted to do. Some people call this desire to praise God an inferiority complex. Once I said, "Praise God," and a man came up to me and said, "Are you inferior?"

I said, "No, I don't think so. I've never been accused of having an inferiority complex."

He said, "Well, why do you say, 'Praise God'?"

I said, "Because He's the one that does it."

His response was: "Do you feel uncomfortable with compliments?"

I said, "No, I don't feel uncomfortable with compliments. I only acknowledge that Jesus, the Father, did it. That's all."

It's hard for us to understand that. Every act of breath, every word, He is the one who gives you strength to say it. That's why it should be easy for us to become aware of His presence.

And Our Lord goes on. He says, "I pray for them" (17:9). Jesus is praying for you. Isn't that phenomenal? Jesus, Son of God, is praying for you. For me. And He said, "I am not praying for the world, but for those you have given me" (17:9). Now, wait a minute.

Does this mean He's not praying for all the non-Christians in the world? No. That is not what Jesus means by "the world." He doesn't mean people in the world; he means worldliness, the evil in the world. He prays for you, for each of us, that we not be put to the test. That was the prayer He gave us to say in the Our Father: "Do not put me to the test, but deliver me from evil." And that's what He said to Peter and James and John in the Garden: "Pray that you are not put to the test" (see Matt. 26:41). But they didn't, and they were tested, and they failed. You know, it's amazing to me that Jesus spent forty days in prayer, whole nights in prayer, and you and I, poor miserable sinners that we are, we think we can go our whole life, day in and day out, without prayer. It's amazing how we think.

"I pray for those you have given me because they belong to you" (17:9). Jesus has been with these men three solid years. I've been with my staff five years, and I'm afraid if I were asked, I'd say they belong to me. But the humility of Jesus is such that He attributes everything to the Father. He said, "Those you have given me, I pray for them because they belong to you." Which means I must love my staff not because they're here, not because they work for me, but because they belong to the Father. I must love you because you belong to the Father, because we're family, because we share the same Father. Our natural fathers are different, but our natural fathers also come from the Father, *the* Father.

Again, He says, "All I have is yours, Father" (see 17:10). These few sentences, verses we call them, are so unselfish that we can't comprehend. And He says, "All you have is mine, and in them I am glorified" (17:10). How is Jesus glorified? By being the Son of God, because He comes from the Father, because everything He does and says is from the Father. "I am not in the world any longer, but they are in the world, and I am coming to you, holy

Father" (see 17:11). Wouldn't it be wonderful if you and I could be so possessed by God that we were aware of the Father's action in every single thing we did? Every single thing.

And He says, "Keep those you have given me true to your name, so they may be one like us" (17:11). That is your dignity, and that, my friends, is your calling. Whether you're married or single, minister, missionary, priest, or religious, you are called by God to an exalted dignity, and it's right here: "Holy Father, keep those you have given me true to your name, so they may be one like us." You and I are to be true to the name of the Father. We are to be true to Him in His Church. We are to be true to the Eucharist. We are to be true to Reconciliation. We are to be true to the spiritual life. We are to be true witnesses that the Father sent Jesus and Jesus is Lord. We ought to be true to our Mother Mary and not push her in some kind of corner because we don't understand her awesome dignity as Mother of God. We're to be true. We are to be holy as God is holy. Don't throw that away for something evil. Don't push it back in the face of God and say, "I don't want to be like You." We may not understand, and we may find it difficult, but just say, "Lord God, Father, I thank You for Your goodness to me. Teach me how to be like Your Son, Jesus, that we, He and I, may glorify Thee in this world." Live in the Trinity. God bless you.

Mother M. Angelica
(1923-2016)

Mother Mary Angelica of the Annunciation was born Rita Antoinette Rizzo on April 20, 1923, in Canton, Ohio. After a difficult childhood, a healing of her recurring stomach ailment led the young Rita on a process of discernment that ended in the Poor Clares of Perpetual Adoration in Cleveland.

Thirteen years later, in 1956, Sr. Angelica promised the Lord as she awaited spinal surgery that, if He would permit her to walk again, she would build Him a monastery in the South. In Irondale, Alabama, Mother Angelica's vision took form. Her distinctive approach to teaching the Faith led to parish talks, then pamphlets and books, then radio and television opportunities.

By 1980 the Sisters had converted a garage at the monastery into a rudimentary television studio. EWTN was born. Mother Angelica has been a constant presence on television in the United States and around the world for more than thirty-five years. Innumerable conversions to the Catholic Faith have been attributed to her unique gift for presenting the gospel: joyful but resolute, calming but bracing.

Mother Angelica's Keys to the Interior Life

Mother Angelica spent the last years of her life cloistered in the second monastery she founded: Our Lady of the Angels in Hanceville, Alabama, where she and her Nuns dedicated themselves to prayer and adoration of Our Lord in the Most Blessed Sacrament.